Simple Stitches

Knits with Textured Details

Eva Wiechmann

Martingale®
& COMPANY

Simple Stitches: Knits with Textured Details
© 2009 by Eva Wiechmann

Martingale®
& C O M P A N Y

Martingale & Company
20205 144th Ave. NE
Woodinville, WA 98072-8478 USA
www.martingale-pub.com

Printed in China
14 13 12 11 10 09   8 7 6 5 4 3 2 1

Library of Congress Cataloging-in-Publication Data
Library of Congress Control Number: 2008054621

ISBN: 978-1-56477-900-7

Mission Statement

Dedicated to providing quality products and service to inspire creativity.

Credits

President & CEO: Tom Wierzbicki
Editor in Chief: Mary V. Green
Managing Editor: Tina Cook
Technical Editor: Ursula Reikes
Copy Editor: Sheila Chapman Ryan
Design Director: Stan Green
Production Manager: Regina Girard
Illustrators: Robin Strobel & Laurel Strand
Cover & Text Designer: Regina Girard
Photographer: Brent Kane

Acknowledgments

Thanks to
Hans and Martha Dankers
for graciously permitting us
to photograph the garments in
this book in their lovely gardens.
Thanks to the Martingale &
Company staff, and special
thanks to Ursula Reikes
for helping me get it right.

Table of Contents

Garter-Stitch Projects

Seed-Stitch Projects

  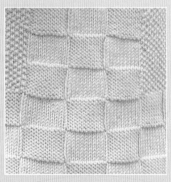 

Ribbing and Cable Projects

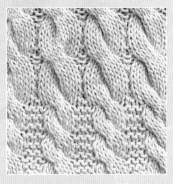

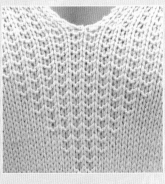

Openwork Projects

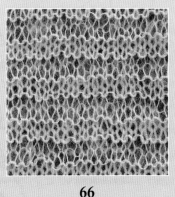

Introduction

knitting should be relaxing

In our increasingly hectic world, knitting should be relaxing. The patterns in this book were designed to do just that—help you relax as you knit. Because these garments are worked with yarns that are soft and luxurious in light, soothing colors, you'll feel like you're on a vacation when you make them. Wonderful details create shaping without the usual increases and decreases. The best part of all is that the patterns require little finishing. Almost everything is joined as you go, picked up, or worked right in. Look out, these sweaters are about to become your favorite pieces. You'll be making them and wearing them for years to come. Enjoy.

Eva

Before You Begin

Most of the sweaters are designed with plenty of ease so that they are very comfortable to wear and aren't tight on the body. Depending on the amount of ease you prefer, one size can be good for several bust measurements. Measure the bust on one of your favorite comfortable sweaters. Use that bust measurement to select the size to make. Measure the length of your favorite sweater as well, since you can easily adjust any of these patterns to that length.

Pattern stitches are used to shape the sweaters and create special effects. When you block your sweater to the finished measurements, pay attention to the pattern stitches. These are areas where you can make minor adjustments to the finished size. Open the stitches up a bit for a looser fit, or let them sit nice and snug for a tighter fit.

pay attention to the pattern stitches

Here is some basic information for new knitters and a few helpful reminders—and perhaps a few new tips—for more experienced knitters.

Gauge

Stitch gauge is very important when knitting a garment. The gauges in this book are given over stockinette stitch rather than the pattern stitch. This will make it faster and easier for you to determine the correct gauge. If you can achieve gauge in stockinette stitch, you will achieve gauge in the pattern stitch. I like to make a large swatch, at least 6" x 6", and block it before measuring the gauge. This may sound like a lot of work, but trust me, it's worth every minute.

Many popular fibers like bamboo, rayon, and microfiber change quite a bit after blocking. So please do yourself a favor and check your gauge if you want your sweater to turn out right. To make adjustments in your gauge if you have too many stitches, go up a needle size; too few stitches, go down a needle size.

Not all patterns include a row gauge. In those cases, the pieces are worked to a specific measurement or for a specific number of pattern rows.

Casting On

For most of the garments, you can use whichever cast on you prefer. However, several garments require a specific cast on to achieve the desired effect.

Knitted Cast On

*Knit into the stitch on the left needle; don't take it off but put it back on the left needle. Repeat from * for required number of stitches.

 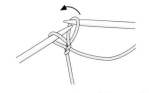

Knit into stitch.   Place new stitch on left needle.

Decorative Cast On

This cast on is similar to the standard long-tail cast on and produces a lovely decorative, yet sturdy, edge.

1. Measure out the required yarn as for the long-tail cast on. Make a slipknot and place the loop on the right needle. Hold the yarn from the ball around the index finger and the tail around the thumb as usual. Now add a second strand of yarn to the tail around the thumb. Hold the end of this second strand of yarn with your little finger.

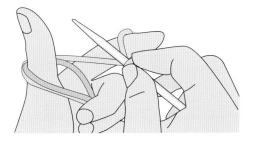

2. *Insert the needle under the double thumb yarn, and then over the yarn around the index finger, and through the thumb loop. Let go of the yarns and tighten gently.

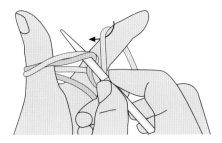

3. Wind the double thumb yarn around the thumb so that the yarns coming from the stitch on the needle are at the *front* of the thumb.

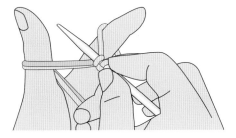

4. Insert the needle under the two back threads of the thumb yarn, and then over the yarn around the index finger, and through the thumb loop. Let go of the yarns and tighten gently.

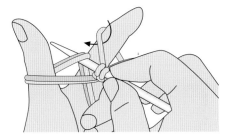

5. Wind the double thumb yarn around the thumb so that the yarns coming from the stitch are at the *back* of the thumb*.

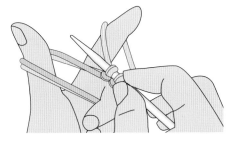

Rep from * to * for required number of stitches.

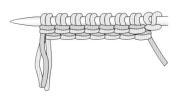

Provisional Crochet-Chain Cast On

With waste yarn (I recommend a smooth cotton in a contrasting color), make a chain that is a few stitches longer than the number of stitches required. Finish off the chain loosely. With your working yarn pick up and knit (or purl) a stitch out of the bump from the back of the chain. When these stitches are needed, remove the waste yarn and put the stitches on a needle.

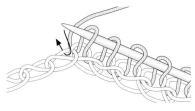

Knit on stitches in
the back of the chain.

Permanent Crochet-Chain Cast On

Work the same as the "Provisional Crochet-Chain Cast On" above, but use working yarn to make the chain and incorporate chains into the pattern.

Cast-On Hints

How much tail should you leave for a long-tail cast on? Use one of these methods to decide.

Guesstimate. Not very reliable but if it works, good.

Wrap method. Wrap the yarn around the needle a set number of times (10 for easy count), measure this length, and multiply by tens for the number of stitches needed.

Use two balls of yarn. Especially good method if you have to cast on a lot of stitches, like many of the sweaters in this book. Make a slipknot with both yarns. Hold one yarn around the thumb and the other around the index finger. At the end of the required number of stitches, cut off the second ball and you are good to go.

Increase and Decreases

One increase and several decreases are used for the patterns in this book.

Make one (M1). This is an almost invisible increase. Pick up the horizontal thread between two stitches from front to back and knit into the back of it. One stitch increased.

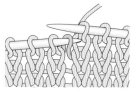

Pick up horizontal strand
between two stitches.

Knit into back of stitch.

Knit two stitches together (K2tog). This is a right-slanting decrease. Insert the needle into two stitches as if to knit and knit them together. One stitch decreased.

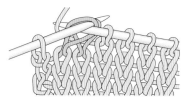

Right slant double decrease (K3tog). Insert the needle into three stitches as if to knit and knit them together. Two stitches decreased.

Slip, slip, knit (ssk). This is a left-slanting decrease. Slip two stitches, one at a time, knitwise, and then insert the left needle from left to right into the front loops and knit the two stitches together. One stitch decreased

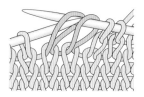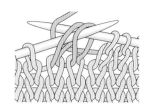

Slip two stitches
to right needle.

Knit two stitches together.

Left slant double decrease (sl2 kw-K1-p2sso). Slip two stitches, one at a time, knitwise, knit one stitch, and then pass the two slipped stitches over the knit stitch. Two stitches decreased.

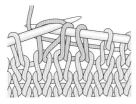 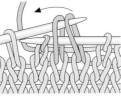

Slip two stitches one at a time as if to knit. Knit the next stitch.

Pass the two slipped stitches over the knit stitch.

Centered double decrease (sl2tog kw-K1-p2sso). Slip two stitches together knitwise, knit one stitch, and then pass the two slipped stitches over the knit stitch. Two stitches decreased.

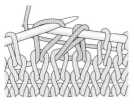 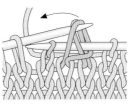

Slip two stitches together as if to knit. Knit the next stitch.

Pass the two slipped stitches over the knit stitch.

Circular Needle Loop Method

For this method, one long circular needle is used to knit a relatively small piece in the round instead of using double-pointed needles or two circular needles. My Mother taught this to me 58 years ago when I first learned to knit. At that time, we did not have many different lengths of needles, so this method was used a lot. It should actually be called "make do with what you have," which is not a bad thing considering the cost of needles today.

This method is particular helpful when picking up sleeve stitches at the shoulders and knitting toward the cuff. As you decrease stitches, you can continue on the same long circular needle. You can use this method in any places that are too tight to knit.

To work this method, pick up the required number of stitches using the long circular needle. Pull out a length of cable about 12 stitches from the right-hand needle so that the needle tips meet.

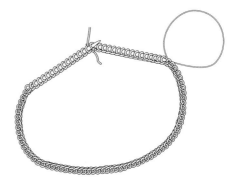

Pull right-hand needle through to make a loop. Push left-hand sts close to the tip. Now you can knit until the space gets tight again.

Work as many stitches as you can before your work gets too tight; then pull the needle and cable through, leaving a loop as before, and work the remaining stitches. It's not the fastest method, but it works!

Helpful Gadgets

You'll need the following items when knitting some of the garments.

Markers

Markers simply make life a lot easier; we can spend more time knitting and less time ripping just because we missed a spot. I like soft rubber markers. They don't pop off easily and roll into the Bermuda Triangle of knitting supplies—along with the sewing needles, tape measures and, oh yes, sock needles! Aren't we always missing one out of the set? I also make my own markers. Just cut a piece of cotton yarn, tie the ends into a knot, and you have a perfect marker. The price is right also.

In patterns that are worked in one piece from front to back, you'll need to mark the row that is the halfway point of the garment. To do this, attach a split stitch marker or tie a piece of yarn at each end of the appropriate row.

Stitch Holders

Stitch holders are used often in these patterns. Since most of the finishing is done with live stitches, some of the work has to be parked for a while until you are ready to join the pieces. Double-ended holders are wonderful because they have points on both ends. No more transferring stitches back and forth—you are good to go in either direction. For a very large number of stitches, use a long circular needle. And then there is the cheap way: slip your stitches onto a smooth length of cotton yarn and tie the ends together. This is also helpful if you want to try your knitting on to see how it is fitting.

Finishing

These garments require very little sewing. The finishing times provided at the end of the garments are approximate and will help the knitter to quickly determine how much finishing actually is involved. This is not a race—we all work at a different pace—but just a reference.

Seams

There are few seams required for these sweaters.

Mattress stitch for stockinette-stitch seams. Place the pieces to be seamed next to each other with right sides facing up. Insert the needle under the horizontal bar between two stitches on the left piece, and then repeat with the the matching row on the right piece. Continue weaving back and forth until the seam is complete. Pull tight every five stitches or so to keep the stitches neat, but do not pull too tightly or you will gather the edge.

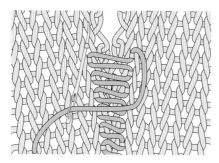

Mattress stitch for reverse-stockinette-stitch and garter-stitch seams. Place the pieces to be seamed next to each other with right sides facing up. Insert the needle into the bottom loop on the left edge, and then into the top loop of the knot on the right edge. Continue weaving back and forth until the seam is complete. Pull tight every five stitches or so to keep the stitches neat, but do not pull too tightly or you will gather the edge.

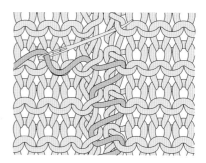

Grafting (Kitchener stitch). Hold the needles together with the right sides facing outward and the working yarn coming from the back needle. Thread yarn on a blunt yarn needle.

1. Insert the needle through the first stitch on the front needle purlwise.

2. Insert the needle through the first stitch on the back needle knitwise; pull yarn through.

3. Insert the needle into the first stitch on the front needle knitwise (take it off but don't pull through yet), insert the needle into the second stitch on the front needle purlwise, and pull your yarn through, leaving the second stitch on the needle. It's one easy motion rather than pulling the yarn twice.

4. Insert the needle into the first stitch on the back needle purlwise (take it off but don't pull through yet), insert the needle into the second stitch on the back needle knitwise, and pull the yarn through, leaving the second stitch on the needle.

Repeat steps 3 and 4 until all stitches are removed.

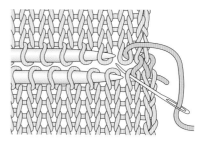

Three-Needle Bind Off (3-Needle BO)

Divide stitches evenly onto two needles and hold with right sides together. With a third needle, knit together one stitch from the front needle and one stitch from the back needle. *Knit together the next stitch on the front and back needles. With two stitches on the right needle, bind off by pulling the second stitch over the first stitch and off the needle. Repeat from * until all stitches are bound off.

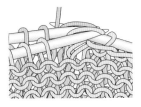
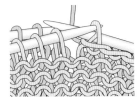

Knit together one stitch from front needle and one stitch from back.

Bind off.

Weaving In Ends

Do it as you go and you won't have a bunch to do at the end. Weave into side seams whenever you can. However, many of the sweaters are worked in one piece or rounds so there are no seams. Carefully weave the ends in so there is nothing showing on the right side. Sections with a change of stitch pattern on the sides or front bands are a good spot to hide yarn ends. Weave ends horizontally on purl rows and vertically on knit rows. For heavier yarns, separate the plies in the yarn and weave the ends in different direcions.

Knitting Zen

Knitting is supposed to be a relaxing experience. To make sure it is, follow a few simple rules.

- Sit comfortably with good back support. Keep your shoulders down and don't forget to breathe.

- Take a break often. Roll your shoulders and flex your fingers. Put your knitting down and talk to your husband. My patterns have plenty of "Honey, you can talk to me now" rows.

- Work with circular needles whenever you can. This way your knitting can rest on your lap and does not put weight on your hands.

- Hold the needles gently. They are *not* that heavy.

- Own a cat. It will make sure that you are taking appropriate breaks.

Tiger helps me relax.

Garter-Stitch Projects

Did you know that the very first stitch you learned can be beautiful? Garter stitch has lots of good qualities. It is reversible, it does not roll at the edges, and it creates interesting shapes when combined with stockinette stitch.

How To

Back and forth. Knit every row for knit garter or purl every row for purl garter.

In the round. Alternate one round of knit and one round of purl throughout.

Buttoned Cardigan, page 16

Simple Top, page 20

Side-to-Side Boatneck Top, page 24

Collared Tunic, page 27

Buttoned Cardigan

Garter stitch is featured at the bottom edge, the shoulders, and the sleeve cuffs. The button bands of alternating garter and stockinette stitch make perfect islands for buttons. The I-cord finish around the neck completes the look.

Skill level: Intermediate ■■■□

Sizes: Small (Medium, Large, Extra Large)

Finished bust: 36 (39, 42, 45)" when buttoned

Finished length: 19 (21½, 23, 23)"

Materials

7 (8, 9, 11) skeins of Calmer from Rowan (75% cotton, 25% acrylic; 50 g; 175 yds/160 m) in color 461 **3**

Size 7 (4.5 mm) circular needle (29" or 32" long) or size to obtain gauge

Size 7 (4.5 mm) double-pointed needle for I-cord bind off (optional)

2 stitch markers

3 stitch holders

4 (4, 5, 5) buttons, ¾" in diameter

Gauge

24 sts and 36 rows = 4" in St st

Note that Calmer has lots of memory, so it pulls in more and has a smaller gauge than you would expect. Pay attention to the gauge rather than the size of yarn if you are substituting.

Body

Sweater is worked in one piece to armholes. Button and buttonhole bands are worked at same time as body.

CO 232 (251, 270, 289) sts.

Bottom Detail

Row 1 (WS): P3, [K10 (11, 12, 13), P2] 18 times, K10 (11, 12, 13), P3.

Row 2 and all RS rows: Knit.

Work rows 1 and 2 a total of 10 (11, 11, 12) times.

Buttonhole Pattern

Row 1 (WS): K13 (14, 15, 16), P38 (41, 44, 47), K10 (11, 12, 13), P1, pm for side seam, P1, K10 (11, 12, 13), P86 (93, 100, 107), K10 (11, 12, 13), P1, pm for side seam, P1, K10 (11, 12, 13), P38 (41, 44, 47), K13 (14, 15, 16).

Row 2 (RS): Knit.

Rows 3–8: Rep last 2 rows 3 times.

Row 9: Rep row 1.

Row 10 (buttonhole row): K3, YO, K2tog, knit to end.

Rows 11–16: Rep rows 1 and 2 above 3 more times.

Button-Band Pattern

Next row (WS): P3, K10 (11, 12, 13), work to 2 sts before marker, P2, sm, P2, work to 2 sts before next marker, P2, sm, P2, work to button band, K10 (11, 12, 13), P3.

Next row: Knit.

Work last 2 rows a total of 10 (11, 11, 12) times; total 20 (22, 22, 24) rows.

Cont working 16-row buttonhole patt alternating with 20 (22, 22, 24) rows of button-band patt, AT THE SAME TIME inc St st portion by 1 st on each side of side markers on first WS row at each change of patt from buttonhole patt to button-band patt. Work until piece measures 11 (12, 13, 13)" from beg, ending with WS row. Note that if you want a longer version of the cardigan, just add more to the body length.

Increases in stockinette stitch at the side create interest.

Buttonholes are created on garter-stitch islands.

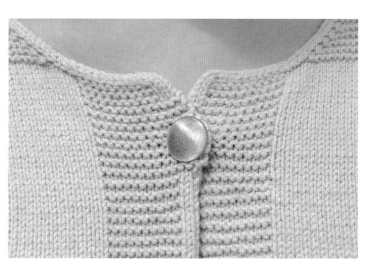

An I-cord bind off finishes the neck nicely .

Divide for back and fronts: On next row, work to first marker, put these sts on holder for right front. BO 6 (7, 8, 8) sts from back. Work to next marker. Turn. Put rem left-front sts on holder. Cont on back, BO 6 (7, 8, 8) sts, K5 (5, 5, 6), including st on your needle, purl to last 5 (5, 5, 6) sts, K5 (5, 5, 6). There will be 96 (103, 110, 119) sts for back and 62 (67, 72, 77) sts for each front.

Back

Next row: Knit.

Working on back, cont in established patt until back measures 8 (9½, 10, 10)" from beg of armhole, ending with RS row. Put sts on holder.

Fronts

Right Front

Next row (WS): With WS facing you, join yarn at armhole and BO 6 (7, 8, 8) sts, K5 (5, 5, 6), which includes last st from BO, purl to front band and work as established (don't forget buttonholes)—56 (60, 64, 69) sts.

Next row: Knit.

Work even in established patt until right front measures 4 (5, 5, 5)" from beg of armhole, ending with WS row.

Shape neck: Work I-cord BO as follows: With RS facing you, *K2, ssk, sl 3 sts from RH needle to LH needle, rep from * to BO a total of 12 (13, 14, 15) sts, then knit to end—44 (47, 50, 54) sts.

Right Shoulder Pattern

Next row (WS): K5 (5, 5, 6), P2, [K10 (11, 12, 13), P2] 3 times, end last rep with P3.

Next row: K3, K2tog, knit to end.

Work last 2 rows 4 more times.

Work even in established patt until front measures same as back, ending with RS row. Put sts on holder.

Left Front

With RS facing you, join yarn at armhole edge and BO 6 (7, 8, 8) sts, knit to end.

Work same as right front (without buttonholes) until piece measures 4 (5, 5, 5)" from beg of armhole, ending with WS row.

Shape neck: Work I-cord BO as follows: With RS facing you, work to last 4 sts, K2tog, K2, do not turn. *Sl 4 sts from RH needle to LH needle, K2tog, K2, do not turn, rep from * to BO a total of 12 (13, 14, 15) sts, knit to end—44 (47, 50, 54) sts.

Left Shoulder Pattern

Next row (WS): P3, [K10 (11, 12, 13), P2] 3 times, K5 (5, 5, 6).

Next row: Knit to last 5 sts, K2tog, K3.

Work last 2 rows 4 more times.

Work even in established patt until left front measures same as back, ending with WS row.

The garter detail is repeated in the shoulders.

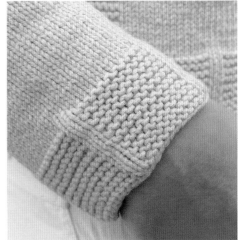

The garter detail is repeated on the cuffs.

Join shoulders: Use 3-needle BO (page 13) to join shoulders, leaving 3 sts from each front on holder. Working with 3 sts from right front, BO back sts using I-cord BO (as for right front above) until you reach 3 sts on left front. Then graft 3 sts of right front tog with sts from left front.

Sleeves

With RS facing you, PU 94 (112, 124, 124) sts along armhole edge, starting from lower inside corner.

Work 7 (7, 9, 9) rows in St st.

Dec row: K2, K2tog, knit to last 4 sts, K2tog, K2. Cont in St st and work dec row on RS rows as follows.

For Small: Work dec row every 6 rows 22 times—50 sts.

For Medium: Work dec row alternating every 4 and 6 rows 29 times—54 sts.

For Large and Extra Large: Work dec row alternating every 4 and 6 rows 33 times—58 sts.

Sleeve should measure approx 16 (17, 18, 18)" from PU row. End with RS row.

Cuff: Work as follows.

Next row (WS): P2, [K10 (11, 12, 12), P2] 4 times.

Next row: Knit.

Work in established patt a total of 19 rows. BO kw.

Finishing

Sew sleeve and underarm seam. Sew on buttons.

Finishing time: Approx 40 minutes.

Block garment to finished measurements.

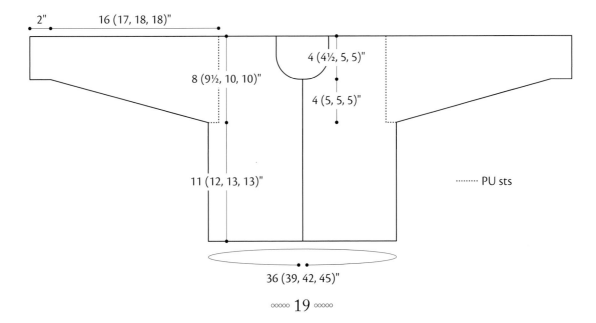

2" 16 (17, 18, 18)"

4 (4½, 5, 5)"

8 (9½, 10, 10)"

4 (5, 5, 5)"

11 (12, 13, 13)"

········ PU sts

36 (39, 42, 45)"

Simple Top

From the bottom edge to the cap sleeve and V-yoke, all the elements of this top follow the triangle theme. Soft bamboo yarn is ideal for the drapey yoke of this shell that can go to work or to an evening out when paired with the right accessories.

Skill level: Easy ◖■□▢

Sizes: Small (Medium, Large)

Finished bust: 34 (37, 40)" in pattern

Finished length: 19 (20, 22)"

Materials

6 (7, 8) skeins of Micro Bamboo from Schachenmayr (50% acrylic, 50% bamboo; 50 g; 145 m/158 yds) in color 105 ②

Size 4 (3.5 mm) needles or size to obtain gauge

2 stitch markers

Gauge

27 sts = 4" in St st

Front

Garment is worked in one piece from front to back.

CO 120 (130, 140) sts. Purl 2 rows.

Bottom Detail

Row 1 (RS): K1, (P8, K2) across, end last rep with K1.

Rows 2, 4, 6, and 8: Purl.

Row 3: K2, (P6, K4) across, end last rep with K2

Row 5: K3, (P4, K6) across, end last rep with K3.

Rows 7 and 9: K4, (P2, K8) across, end last rep with K4.

Row 10: Purl.

Body

Beg St st and cont until piece measures 9½ (9½, 10½)" from beg, ending with WS row. On last row, P59 (64, 69), pm, P2, pm, P59 (64, 69). Markers indicate center of yoke.

Read through yoke and cap sleeve directions before beg yoke; some rows are worked AT THE SAME TIME.

Yoke

Knit to first marker, sm, YO, P2, remove next marker, YO, pm, knit to end. On next row (and all WS rows for yoke), purl across, dropping the YOs. On next RS row, knit to 1 st before marker, pm, YO, P1, remove marker, P1, YO, P1, remove marker, P1, YO, pm, knit to end. Cont to inc yoke patt as established by 2 sts on EOR until 40 (50, 50) sts have been worked into patt. Then on next RS row, work to 3 sts from first marker, P3, BO 40 (50, 50) sts loosely, P3, work to end.

The triangle theme starts at the bottom edge.

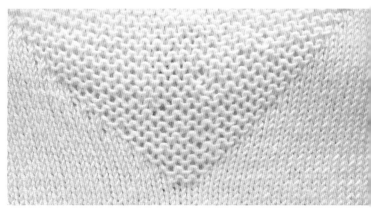

The yoke pattern continues the triangle theme.

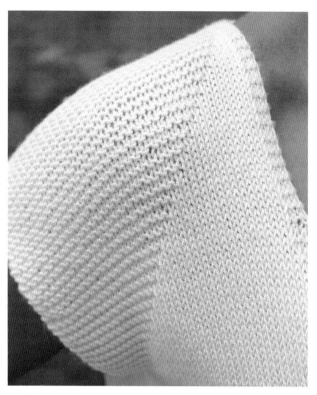

Garter-stitch triangles are worked across the shoulders.

Cap Sleeves

AT THE SAME TIME, when work measures 11
(11½, 12½)", start patt for cap sleeve. On next RS
row, P2 at beg and end of row. On next RS row, P3
at beg and end of row. Cont in this manner, working 1 more purl st at each end on every RS row.
AT THE SAME TIME, after neck BO, on next
WS row, join another ball of yarn for left shoulder.
Keeping 3 sts at each neck edge in purl garter, cont
working 1 more purl st for cap sleeve as above until
piece measures 19 (20, 22)" from beg. Mark last row
as halfway point.

Back

Work to neck, use permanent crochet ch CO (page 10)
to CO 40 (50, 50) sts, cut second yarn and work
across row to join pieces—120 (130, 140) sts.

On cap sleeve patt, start reducing number of purl sts at
each side by 1 st on every RS row. AT THE SAME
TIME on next 8 rows, work first 37 (37, 42) sts in
established patt, work next 46 (56, 56) of back neck
in purl garter, work in established patt to end of row.

Cont cap sleeve in established patt and work back in
St st. When sleeve sts are down to 2 purl sts at each
end, cont in St st and work to same length as front
from halfway point to beg of bottom detail, ending
with WS row.

On next RS row, beg bottom detail with row 9 and cont
patt to row 1.

Purl 1 row. BO pw.

Finishing

Sew side seams.

Finishing time: Approx 25 minutes.

Block garment to finished measurements.

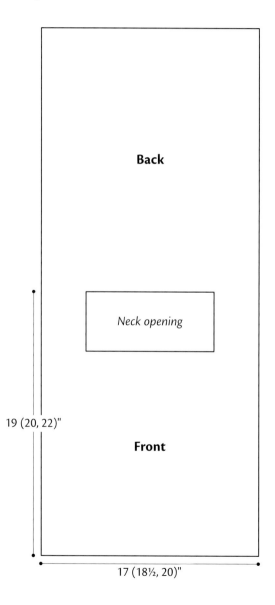

Side-to-Side Boatneck Top

This simple boatneck sweater, worked from side to side,
features alternating garter stitches that create vertical-looking ribbing.

Skill level: Easy ◼◼◻◻

Sizes: Small (Medium, Large, Extra Large)

Finished bust: 37 (40, 44, 48)"

Finished length: 18¼ (18½, 23½, 25)"

Materials

6 (7, 8, 8) skeins of Sublime from Sirdar (75% extra fine merino, 20% silk, 5% cashmere; 50 g; 116 m/127 yds) in color 5 ❸

Size 6 (4 mm) circular needle (29" long) or size to obtain gauge

Size 8 (5 mm) circular needle (29" long)

Size G/6 (4 mm) crochet hook

2 stitch markers

Length of smooth cotton yarn for provisional cast on

Gauge

22 sts and 32 rows = 4" in St st on smaller needle

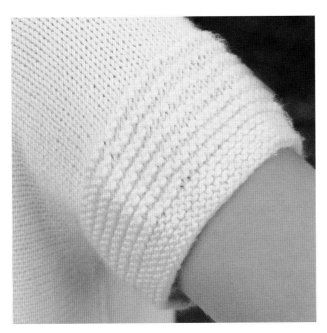

The garter-stitch detail worked on the sleeve

Left Sleeve

Garment is worked from side to side beginning at left sleeve.

With smaller needle, CO 66 (66, 78, 82) sts. Knit 9 rows.

Change to larger needle and knit 14 (14, 18, 18) rows.

Body

Change to smaller needle. With smooth cotton yarn and using provisional crochet ch CO (page 10), CO 67 (70, 90, 96) sts at beg of next 2 rows for front and back—200 (206, 258, 274) sts.

Work in St st, keeping 10 (10, 12, 12) sts at each end in garter st, for 3½ (4, 4¾, 5½)", ending with RS row. On last row K95 (98, 124, 132), pm, K10, pm, K95 (98, 124, 132).

Full Neck Pattern

Row 1 (WS): K10, purl to marker, K10, purl to last 10 sts, K10.

Row 2: Knit.

Row 3: K10, purl to 5 sts before marker, K20, purl to last 10 sts, P10.

Row 4: Knit.

Rep these 4 rows a total of 3 times.

Divide for neck: K100 (103, 129, 137), join second ball of yarn and knit across. Working with 2 separate balls of yarn, work half neck patt (on divided sts).

Half Neck Pattern

Row 1 (WS): K10, purl to marker, K5, with second ball K5, purl to last 10 sts, K10.

Row 2: Knit.

Row 3: K10, purl to 5 sts before marker, K10, with second ball K10, purl to last 10 sts, K10.

Row 4: Knit.

Cont in established patt until neck opening measures 8½ (9, 9½, 10)", ending with WS row.

On next row, join work by working across all sts and cutting second ball. Work full neck patt on page 25 a total of 3 times.

Cont in St st to match the beg, keeping 10 (10, 12, 12) sts at each end in garter st.

Join seam on right-hand side: Turn work inside out. Using 3-needle BO (page 13), BO 67 (70, 90, 96) sts for side seam.

Right Sleeve

Change to larger needle and working on sleeve sts, knit 14 (14, 18, 18) rows. Note that working on the sleeve will be a little tight in the beg. Try using the "Circular Needle Loop Method" on page 11 to make this easier.

Change to smaller needle, knit 9 rows. BO all sts.

Finishing

Transfer sts from provisional CO to needles. Use 3-needle BO to join seam on left-hand side.

Sew little underarm seam.

Finishing time: Approx 10 minutes.

Block garment to finished measurements.

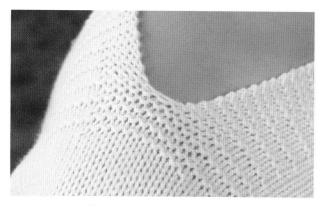

The vertical-looking ribbing at the neck

Full neck pattern before the divide

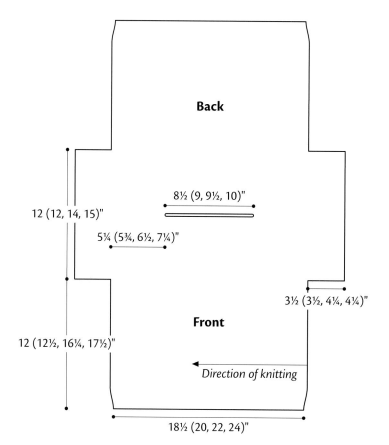

Back

8½ (9, 9½, 10)"

12 (12, 14, 15)"

5¼ (5¾, 6½, 7¼)"

3½ (3½, 4¼, 4¼)"

Front

12 (12½, 16¼, 17½)"

Direction of knitting

18½ (20, 22, 24)"

Collared Tunic

Dress up a long skirt or pair of slacks with this very comfy sweater. The two sizes will fit a wide range of bust measurements. The fake raglan pattern adds interesting and flattering detail. The loose-fitting cowl neck can be buttoned up or left open.

Skill level: Easy ■■□□

Sizes: Small/Medium (Large/Extra Large)

Finished bust: 44 (48)"

Finished back length: 22 (24½)"

Materials

11 (14) skeins of Dolly from Bollicine (100% merino wool; 50 g; 140 m/153 yds) in color 2 (■3■)

Size 7 (4.5 mm) circular needle (29" or 32" long) or size to obtain gauge

Size 9 (6 mm) circular needle (29" or 32" long)

Crochet hook, size G/6 (4 mm)

4 stitch markers

2 buttons, 1" in diameter

Gauge

21 sts = 4" in St st on smaller needle

Back and Front

Garment is worked in one piece from front to back.

With smaller needle, hold 2 strands of yarn tog for thumb yarn and using decorative CO (page 9), CO 116 (126) sts. Cut second strand of thumb yarn.

Garter Border

Every row: Sl 1 pw wyif, knit to last st, K1tbl.

Work garter border for 3".

Body

Beg St st and work until piece measures 14 (16)" from beg or until desired length to underarm.

Sleeves

Using provisional crochet ch CO (page 10), CO 80 (75) at beg of next 2 rows for sleeves—276 (276) sts.

Next RS row: K16, pm, K64 (59), pm, P10, K96 (106), pm, P10, K64 (59), pm, K16.

Next WS row: K16, purl to last marker, K16.

Next RS row: Knit to second marker (at armhole), remove marker, K1, pm, P10, knit to 1 st before next marker, pm, P1, remove marker, P9, knit to end.

Cont in this manner, keeping first and last 16 sts in garter st, and moving raglan patt inward by 1 st on every knit row until sleeve measures 8 (8½)" from CO, ending with WS row.

Neck opening: On next RS row, work first 112 sts in established patt, K52 with waste yarn, put these sts just worked back on LH needle and knit them again with main yarn, finish row in established patt. Mark this row as halfway point.

Cont in established patt, but move the raglan patt out toward the sides by 1 st until sleeve measures 8 (8½)" from halfway point. The number of rows should match beg half of sleeves, ending at the same point.

Join sleeve seams: Remove waste yarn, put sts on needle, turn garment inside out and join sleeve seams with 3-needle BO (page 13) on next 2 rows.

Cont in St st until work measures same as front to garter border. Work 3" of garter border to match front. With 2 strands of yarn held tog, BO pw loosely.

The garter stitch along the bottom border

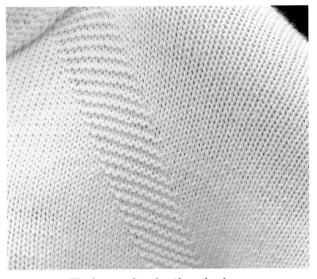

The faux raglan detail on the sleeves

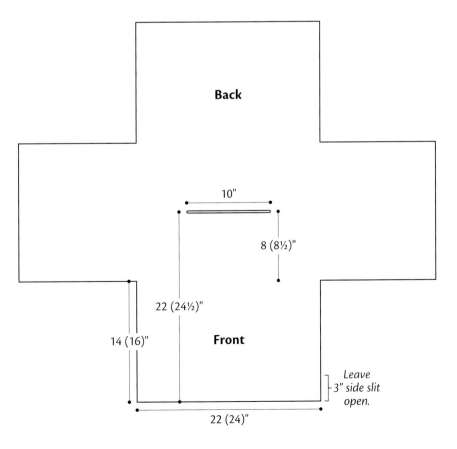

The collar can be buttoned or left open.

Finishing

Collar: Remove waste yarn and place sts on smaller needle. Join yarn at left shoulder, PU 2 sts at each shoulder and work garter st in rnds starting with purl rnd. Work garter st in the rnd for 2". Change to larger needle and cont in garter st, working back and forth for 2½". With 2 strands of yarn held tog, BO pw loosely.

Sc around collar opening, making 2 ch loops on left edge of collar to accommodate size of buttons. Sew on buttons.

Sew up side seams, leaving garter border open.

Finishing time: Approx 40 minutes.

Block garment to finished measurements.

Back

10"

8 (8½)"

22 (24½)"

14 (16)"

Front

Leave
3" side slit
open.

22 (24)"

Seed-Stitch Projects

Seed stitch is a lovely reversible stitch with a wonderful texture that makes most yarns shine. It looks like strings of pearls. The German word for seed stitch is perlmuster, which translates literally to "pearl pattern."

How To

Back and forth. (Over an even number of sts.)
Row 1: *K1, P1, rep from *.
Row 2: *P1, K1, rep from *.

Back and forth. (Over an odd number of sts.)
Every row: K1, *P1, K1, rep from *.

In the round. (Over an even number of sts.)
Rnd 1: *K1, P1, rep from *.
Rnd 2: *P1, K1, rep from *.

In the round. (Over an odd number of sts.)
Rnd 1: K1, *P1, K1, rep from *.
Rnd 2: P1, *K1, P1, rep from *.

Comfy Short-Sleeved Tunic, page 32

Casual Jacket, page 35

Casual Top, page 39

A-Line Tunic, page 42

Comfy Short-Sleeved Tunic

This relaxed tunic is the perfect "Don't have to suck your tummy in" sweater. A combination of seed stitches and smooth stockinette stitches at the bottom edge creates an interesting wave pattern. The sleeve and neck patterns are worked at the same time, which makes finishing a breeze.

Skill level: Intermediate ◖■■▢

Sizes: Small (Medium, Large, Extra Large)

Finished bust: 37 (40, 43, 46)" in pattern

Finished length: 20 (21½, 23½, 24½)"

Materials

8 (9, 10, 11) skeins of Catania from Schachenmayr (100% cotton; 50 g; 125 m/136 yds) in color 105 **〖3〗**

Size 4 (3.5 mm) needles or size to obtain gauge

2 stitch markers

2 stitch holders

Gauge

24 sts and 34 rows = 4" in St st

Back

CO 115 (125, 135, 145) sts.

Bottom Detail

Row 1 (RS): (P1, K1, P1, K1, P1, K5) across to last 5 sts, end P1, K1, P1, K1, P1.

Row 2: (P1, K1, P1, K1, P1, P5) across to last 5 sts, end P1, K1, P1, K1, P1.

Work rows 1 and 2 a total of 10 times.

Body

Beg St st and cont until piece measures 13 (14, 15½, 16½)", ending with WS row. AT THE SAME TIME work seed-st relief patts by working 15–19 sts in seed st for 2 rows randomly across rows. Work these random patts every 6 to 8 rows. I call these my wake-up rows. They make it more interesting.

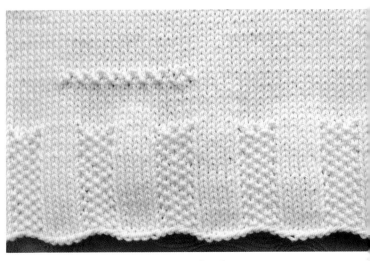

Bottom detail

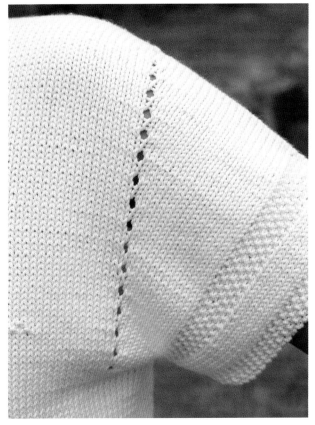

Sleeve detail

Sleeves

Using knitted CO (page 9), CO 10 sts at beg of next 2 rows—135 (145, 155, 165) sts. Work sleeve patt beg on next RS row as follows.

Row 1 (inc row): (P1, K1, P1, K1, P1, K5) twice, YO, pm, knit to last 20 sts, pm, YO, (K5, P1, K1, P1, K1, P1) twice.

Row 2: Work established patt, purling YOs.

Rows 3 and 4: Work established patt without YOs.

Cont to work rows 1–4, adding 1 st to each sleeve every 4 rows, by working YO before first marker and YO after second marker until 14 (15, 16, 16) incs have been made on each sleeve—163 (175, 187, 197) sts. Just count the holes.

Neck Patt: Cont in established patt across 56 (62, 66, 71) sts, work next 51 (51, 55, 55) sts in seed st, finish row in established patt. Rep last row 5 times. On next RS row, work in established patt across 61 (67, 71, 76) sts, BO 41 (41, 45, 45) sts, finish row in established patt. Add second ball of yarn, working both sides at same time, and keeping 5 seed sts on each side of neck, work 8 more rows in established patt. Put all sts on holders.

Front

Work same as back, but start neck patt when 9 (10, 11, 11) incs have been made on each sleeve—153 (165, 177, 187) sts. On next RS row, work across 51 (57, 61, 66) sts, work next 51 (51, 55, 55) sts in seed st,

Detail of the side slit

finish row in established patt. Work neck same as back, cont in patt until piece measures the same; remember to cont sleeves incs to 14 (15, 16, 16) sts on each sleeve. Join sleeve cap and shoulders with Kitchener stitch (page 12).

Finishing

Sew underarm seams. Sew side seams, leaving 2½" side slits at bottom edges.

Finishing time: Approx 50 minutes if you count the Kitchener st.

Block garment to finished measurements.

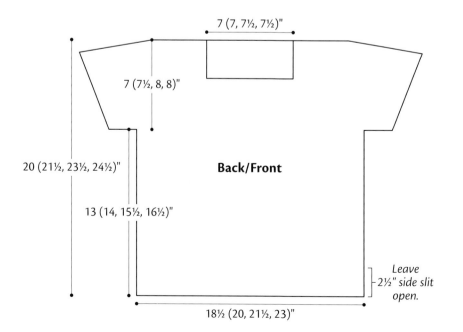

Casual Jacket

Seed-stitch details are used in combination with stockinette- and garter-stitch squares to create a comfortable jacket suitable for every day. The little pink trim and hidden pink pockets make this jacket special. Pair the jacket with the Casual Top (page 39) to create a harmonious outfit.

Skill level: Intermediate ■■■□

Sizes: Small/Medium (Large, Extra Large)

Finished bust: 39 (47, 55)" in pattern

Finished length: 23 (26, 27)"

Materials

MC 11 (13, 15) skeins of Merino Big from Lana Grossa (100% wool; 50 g; 120 m/130 yds) in color 616 grey ④

CC 1 skein of Extra Soft Merino from Gedifra (100% wool; 50 g; 105 m/114 yds) in color 9157 pink ④

Size 8 (5mm) circular needle (29" or 32" long) or size to obtain gauge

5 stitch holders

Gauge

20 sts = 4" in St st

Stitch Patterns

Seed stitch. See page 30.

Block Pattern (over even number of blocks)
Back and Forth

Rows 1, 3, 5, 7, and 9: *K10, P10, rep from *.

Rows 2, 4, 6, 8, and 10: Knit the knit sts and purl the purl sts as they face you.

Rows 11, 13, 15, 17, and 19: *P10, K10, rep from *.

Rows 12, 14, 16, 18, and 20: Knit the knit sts and purl the purl sts as they face you.

Rep rows 1–20.

In the Round

Rnds 1–10: *K10, P10, rep from *.

Rnds 11–20: *P10, K10, rep from *.

Rep rnds 1–20.

Block Pattern (over odd number of blocks)
Back and Forth

Rows 1, 3, 5, 7, and 9: K10, *P10, K10, rep from *.

Rows 2, 4, 6, 8, and 10: Knit the knit sts and purl the purl sts as they face you.

Rows 11, 13, 15, 17, and 19: P10, *K10, P10, rep from *.

Rows 12, 14, 16, 18, and 20: Knit the knit sts and purl the purl sts as they face you.

Rep rows 1–20.

In the Round

Rnds 1–10: K10, *P10, K10, rep from *.

Rnds 11–20: P10 *K10, P10, rep from *.

Rep rnds 1–20.

Pocket Lining (make 2)

With CC, CO 20 sts and work in St st for 4". Put sts on holder.

Body

Jacket is worked in one piece to armhole.

With MC, CO 200 (240, 280) sts. Work seed st for 4".

Join pockets and start body patt: Work 20 sts in established seed st, drop MC, with CC BO kw next 20 sts and cut CC, pick up MC and work block patt across pocket lining, work 120 (160, 200) sts in block patt, drop MC, with CC BO next 20 sts kw and cut CC, pick up MC and work block patt across sts from pocket lining, work 20 sts in established seed st. Keeping first and last 20 sts in seed st, work block patt until piece measures 14 (16, 16½)" or desired length. End with WS row.

Divide for back and fronts: Work 50 (60, 70) sts in established patt. Put these sts on holder for right front. BO 5 sts, work next 5 sts in seed st, work 90 (110, 130) sts in established block patt, turn. Put rem 50 (60, 70) sts on holder for left front. Turn.

Back

BO 5 sts, work 5 sts in seed st, cont established block patt to last 5 sts, end 5 sts in seed st—90 (110, 130) sts for back.

Cont in established patt until armhole measures 5½ (6½, 7)", ending with WS row.

Back seed-st detail: Work in established patt across 35 (45, 55) sts, work center 20 sts in seed st, finish row in established patt. Cont in established patt and on every row, inc seed-st patt by 1 st on each side of center seed-st patt until 40 sts have been worked into seed st.

Cont even in established patt until armhole measures 8 (9, 9½)", ending with WS row.

On next row: Work in established patt across 25 (35, 45) sts, put 40 center sts on holder, join second ball of yarn and finish row in established patt.

Work 5 rows in seed st on rem sts for each shoulder. Put sts on holder.

Fronts

Left Front

With RS facing you, join yarn at armhole edge front. BO 5 sts—45 (55, 65) sts. Work 5 sts in seed st, work established block patt over 20 (30, 40) sts, work 20 sts in seed st at front edge. Work in established patt until armhole measures 8 (9, 9½)", ending with RS row.

On next WS row, BO 20 sts for collar. Work 5 rows of seed st on rem sts for shoulder.

Right Front

With WS facing you, join yarn at armhole edge and work 5 sts in seed st, then cont in established patt across row. Work until armhole measures 8 (9, 9½)", ending with WS row.

The pockets outlined in a contrasting color

The seed-stitch detail at the armholes

The seed-stitch detail along the back neck

On next RS row, BO 20 sts for collar. Work 5 rows of seed st on rem sts for shoulder.

Join shoulders with 3-needle BO (page 13).

Sleeves

With RS facing you, PU 90 (90, 100) sts, starting from lower inside corner.

Work block patt for 10".

Work seed st for 4".

BO in patt.

Finishing

Collar trim: With CC and starting at right collar, PU and BO 20 sts purlwise at same time. From holder for back neck, knit and BO 40 sts knitwise at same time. At left collar, PU and BO 20 sts purlwise at same time. Turn flaps of collar over to right side.

Sew up underarm and sleeve seams.

Sew pocket linings inside the fronts.

Finishing time: Approx 30 minutes.

Block garment to finished measurements.

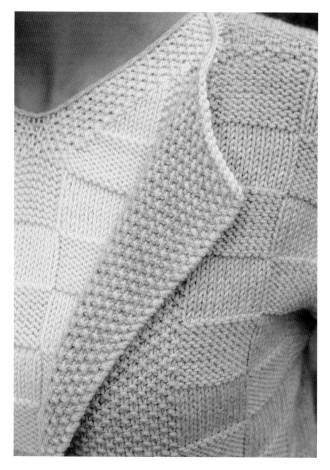

The collar with contrasting trim

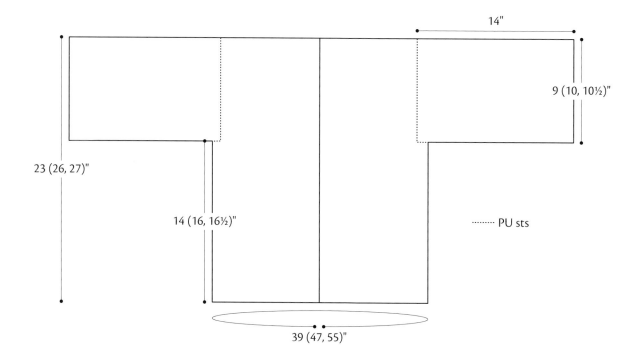

14"

9 (10, 10½)"

23 (26, 27)"

14 (16, 16½)"

·········· PU sts

39 (47, 55)"

Casual Top

This top, with its matching patterns and gray trim, is the perfect companion to the Casual Jacket (page 35). You could also wear it as a vest for layering.

Skill level: Easy ◼◼☐☐

Sizes: Small (Medium, Large, Extra Large)

Finished bust: 35 (39, 43, 47)" in pattern

Finished length: 19½ (20½, 22½, 23½)"

Materials

6 (7, 7, 8) skeins of Extra Soft Merino from Gedifra (100% merino wool; 50 g; 120 m/130 yds) in color 9157 ◀4▶

1 skein of Merino Big from Lana Grossa (100% wool; 50 g; 120 m/130 yds) in color grey ◀4▶

Size 8 (5 mm) circular needle (29" or 32" long) or size to obtain gauge

2 stitch holders

1 stitch marker

Gauge

18 sts = 4" in St st

Stitch Patterns

Seed stitch. See page 30.

Block pattern. See page 36.

Body

Top is worked in the round to armholes.

With CC CO 180 (200, 220, 240) sts, pm and join into rnd. Cut CC. Join MC, work block patt 9 (10, 11, 12) times. Work 30 rnds in block patt.

The block pattern at the bottom edge

Next rnd: Work 30 (30, 40, 40) sts in seed st, work 30 (40, 30, 40) sts in established block patt, work 60 (60, 80, 80) sts in seed st, work 30 (40, 30, 40) sts in established block patt, work 30 (30, 40, 40) sts in seed st.

Work in established patt until piece measures 11 (12, 13, 14)" from beg.

Divide for back and front: Place next 90 (100, 110, 120) sts on holder for front. Cont on 90 (100, 110, 120) back sts. Block patt should be centered on front and back, with equal number of seed sts on each side.

Back

Shape armhole: Work 3 seed sts, K3tog, work established patt to last 6 sts, K3tog, work 3 seed sts. Turn. Work in established patt to end. Work dec at armholes EOR a total of 4 (4, 6, 6) times—74 (84, 86, 96) sts. Work even until armhole measures 6½ (6½, 7½, 7½)".

Work 5 rows of seed st across all sts. On first row: work 36 (41, 42, 47) sts in established patt, K2tog, finish row.

Shape neck: Work 20 (23, 23, 28) sts in established patt, BO center 33 (37, 39, 39) sts. Join second ball of yarn and finish row. Work 5 rows of seed st on 20 (23, 23, 28) sts for each shoulder. Put shoulder sts on st holders.

Front

Place front sts on needle. With WS facing you, join yarn at armhole. Work in established patt to end. Work armhole dec on next row and EOR as for back. Cont even until armhole measures 2½ (2½, 3½, 3½)". On last row, work 32 (37, 38, 43) sts in patt, pm, work 10 sts, pm, finish row. Cont in established patt, but work 10 sts between markers in seed st for 2 rows.

Shape neck: Work 37 (42, 43, 48) sts, drop yarn but do not cut, join second ball of yarn in next st and work to end of row. Work one WS row in established patt. On next RS row, with first ball of yarn, work in patt to 6 sts from end of first half, K2tog, work 4 seed sts, with second ball of yarn, work 4 seed sts, K2tog, work in established patt to end. Rep dec on EOR a total of 13 (15, 16, 16) times. Then dec 2 sts at each neck as follows: Work to 7 sts from end of first half, K3tog, work 4 seed sts; for second half, work 4 seeds sts, K3tog, finish row. Rep this dec EOR a total of 2 times.

Work even until front measures same as back.

Finishing

Join shoulders with 3-needle BO (page 13).

Neck trim (optional): With RS facing you and CC, PU and BO sts at neck at same time.

Finishing time: Approx 15 minutes for neck trim but no sewing.

Block garment to finished measurements.

Detail of the V-neck pattern and contrasting trim

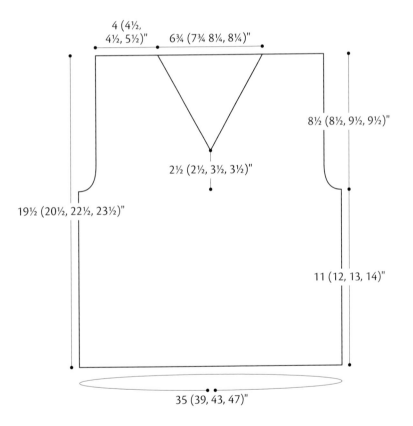

A-Line Tunic

This sweater is roomy but has a slight feminine taper that is created by decreases and increases in the pattern stitches. The two sizes are ample, and will look good on every body.

Skill level: Easy ◼️◼️☐☐

Sizes: Small/Medium (Large/Extra Large)

Finished bust: 39 (44)" in pattern just below armhole

Finished length: 23 (25½)"

Materials

17 (19) skeins of Tajmahal from GGH (70% merino, 22% silk, 8% cashmere; 25 g; 85 m/92 yds) in color 33 ice blue **②**

3 size 5 (3.75 mm) circular needles (20", 29", and 32" long) or size to obtain gauge. Use the 29"-long needle to hold stitches while working on sleeves.

5 stitch markers

4 stitch holders

Gauge

26 sts and 32 rows = 4" in St st

Body

Body is worked in the round to armholes.

Holding 2 strands of yarn over thumb, use decorative CO (page 9) to CO 280 (320) sts. Cut second strand of thumb yarn. Pm and join into rnd, being careful not to twist stitches.

Rnd 1: (P1, K1, P1, K17) 14 (16) times.

Rnd 2: (K1, P1, K1, K17) 14 (16) times.

Work last 2 rnds a total of 7 (8) times. On last rnd, work to 1 st before marker, sl next st to right needle, remove marker, sl st back to left needle, replace marker at new beg of rnd. You have moved the marker 1 st to the right, and will now add 2 seed sts and dec 2 knit sts on each rep on next rnd.

Rnd 1: (K1, P1, K1, P1, K1, K15) around.

Rnd 2: (P1, K1, P1, K1, P1, K15) around.

Work last 2 rnds a total of 7 (8) times. On last rnd, rep moving marker as above.

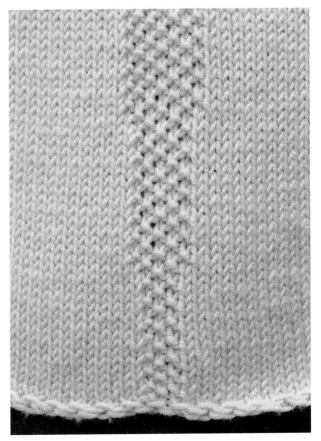

The seed-stitch detail starts at the bottom edge.

Cont patt in this manner, inc number of seed sts and dec number of knit sts every 14 (16) rnds, moving marker on last rnd as above, until you have (17 seed sts, K3) for next 14 (16) rnds.

Next rnd (dec): (work 17 seed sts, sl2tog kw-K1-p2sso) around—252 (288) sts.

Work 1 rnd even in established patt (17 seed sts, K1).

Next 7 rnds: Dec number of seed sts and inc number of knit sts by 1 st at each side of patt section until you have 3 seed sts, 15 knit sts for patt. You will be moving marker to the left by 1 st. At end of seventh rnd, marker is back to original place.

Work even in established patt for 1½ (2)".

Armholes: Work first 8 sts in established patt, put last 11 sts just worked (including 3 sts from before beg of rnd marker) on holder for underarm. Cont in established patt across next 126 (144) sts, put last 11 sts just worked on holder for second underarm. Cont to end of rnd. Leave sts on needle for now.

Sleeves

Using another needle and 2 strands of yarn over thumb, use decorative CO to CO 61 sts. Cut second strand of thumb yarn. Purl next row (WS).

Row 1 (RS): K5, (P1, K9) 5 times, P1, K5.

Row 2: Purl.

Work last 2 rows a total of 4 times.

Next row (RS): K4, (P1, K1, P1, K7) 5 times, P1, K1, P1, K4.

Next row: P4, (P1, K1, P1, P7) 5 times, P1, K1, P1, K4.

Work last 2 rows a total of 4 times.

Next row: K3, (K1, P1, K1, P1, K1, K5) 5 times, K1, P1, K1, P1, K1, K3.

Next row: P3, (K1, P1, K1, P1, K1, P5) 5 times, K1, P1, K1, P1, K1, P3.

Work last 2 rows a total of 4 times.

Next row: K2, (P1, K1, P1, K1, P1, K1, P1, K3) 5 times, P1, K1, P1, K1, P1, K1, P1, K2.

Next row: P2, (P1, K1, P1, K1, P1, K1, P1, P3) 5 times, P1, K1, P1, K1, P1, K1, P1, P2.

Work last 2 rows a total of 4 times.

Next row: K1, (K1, P1, K1, P1, K1, P1, K1, P1, K1, K1) 5 times, K1, P1, K1, P1, K1, P1, K1, P1, K2.

Next row: P1, (K1, P1) 30 times.

Work last 2 rows a total of 4 times.

Next row: (P1, K9) 6 times, P1.

Next row: Purl.

Work last 2 rows for sleeve patt, and inc 1 st at each end on next and every 8th row a total of 12 (18) times, incorporating inc sts into patt—85 (97) sts.

Work even until sleeve measures 17 (18)".

Put first 6 and last 5 sts on holder for right sleeve, first 5 and last 6 sts on holder for left sleeve.

The seed-stitch detail

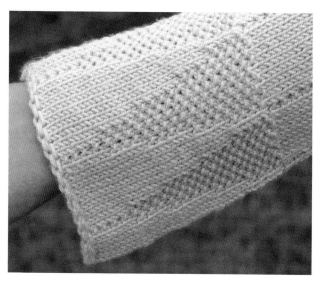

The cuff includes similar seed-stitch details.

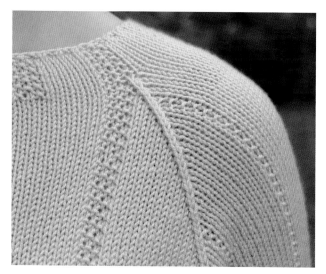

Close-up of raglan and neck details

Join Sleeves to Body

With RS facing you, and keeping established patts for sleeves and body, work across right sleeve, pm, work across back, pm, work across left sleeve, pm, work across front, pm—378 (438) sts. Join and work 1 row in established patt (see "Circular Needle Loop Method" on page 11).

Next rnd (raglan dec): (Work to 1 st before marker, sl2tog kw–K1-p2sso) around. Remove marker and replace it if you wish to before the dec st (you probably won't need markers as the decs become visible).

Next rnd: Work even in patt.

Rep last 2 rnds for raglan dec until you have 15 sts on sleeves and 57 sts each on front and back.

Finishing

Neckband: Using 20"-long circular needle, (K6, 3 seed sts) around, matching the prev patt. Work 1" (or more if you prefer a higher collar). BO in patt.

Sew sleeve seam. Graft 11 underarm sts to 11 rem sleeve sts using Kitchener st (page 12).

Finishing time: Approx 35 minutes.

Block garment to finished measurements

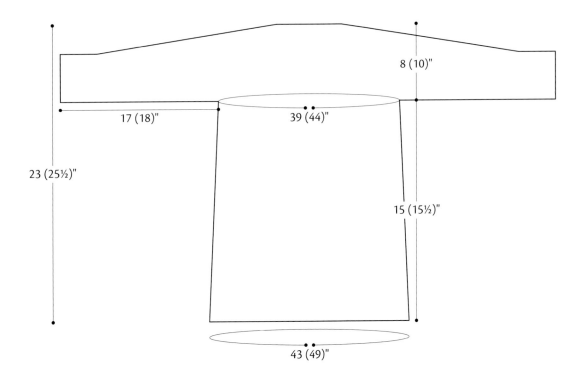

8 (10)"

17 (18)"

39 (44)"

23 (25½)"

15 (15½)"

43 (49)"

Ribbing and Cable Projects

Ribbings and cables can be used to create wonderful shaping. You can nip and tuck with them. You can create vertical, slimming lines or move them diagonally or horizontally for some interesting textures. Keep the numbers and repeats simple and you won't have a problem.

How To

Ribbings. Ribbings are created by working a repeat of knits and purls. They can be regular repeats like K1, P1 or K4, P4, or they can be irregular repeats like K8, P1.

Cables. Cables are created when the stitches are crossed at regular intervals. For example, the six-stitch cable used in the Cabled Summer Top (page 57) is crossed every six rows. The eight-stitch cable is crossed every twelve rows.

Cashmere Swing Coat, page 48

Three-Directional Pullover, page 53

Cabled Summer Top, page 57

Easy Breezy Top, page 61

Cashmere Swing Coat

Every knitter should experience working with luxury yarn like cashmere at least once. This flattering ribbed and smocked swing jacket is simply heavenly.

Skill level: Intermediate ■■■□

Sizes: Small/Medium (Large/Extra Large)

Finished bust: 39 (44)" in pattern

Finished length: 27 (29)"

Materials

11 (12) skeins of 4-ply Mongolian Cashmere from Jade Sapphire (100% Mongolian cashmere; 55 g; 200 yds) in color 01 ②

Size 5 (3.75 mm) circular needle or size to obtain gauge (a 47"-long Addi lace needle works well)

2 buttons, 1¼" diameter

3 stitch holders

4 stitch markers

Gauge

26 sts = 4" in St st

Stitch Pattern

Smock Stitch: YO, K2, P2, K2, pull YO up and over 6 sts just worked.

Body

Body is worked in one piece to armholes.

Knit first and last st of every row unless otherwise instructed.

CO 376 (408) sts (see "Using two balls of yarn" in "Cast-On Hints" on page 10).

Row 1 (WS): K1, (P2, K2) 5 times, (P6, K2) 4 (5) times, P6, pm, (K2, P2) 20 times, pm, K2, (P6, K2) 12 (14) times, pm, (P2, K2) 20 times, pm, (P6, K2) 5 (6) times, (P2, K2) 4 times, end with P2, K1.

Row 2: Keeping first and last st as K1 on every row, knit the knit sts and purl the purl sts as they face you.

Rep rows 1 and 2 for 3 (5)", ending with WS row.

Smock patt: Smock patt is worked over 80 sts between markers on each side. On first RS row, work to first marker, *(P2, K2) 7 times, P2, (smock, P2) 3 times, (P2, K2) 7 times, sl next marker*, work to next marker and rep from * to *. Work in established patt to end of row. Cont smock patt over 80 sts, referring to chart on page 52.

Buttonhole: AT THE SAME TIME when work measures 14½ (16½)", work on WS row to last 12 sts, join second ball of yarn and work 10 rows in patt , keeping 1 st at each buttonhole edge in garter st. Join work again after 10 rows and cut extra yarn. Work second buttonhole same way, 3" from first one.

Back view of the swing coat

A button in a vertical buttonhole

The smock stitch on the back shoulder

Divide for back and fronts: Work until piece measures 16½ (18½)" from beg, ending with RS row.

On next WS row, work to first marker, *K2, (P2, K2) 3 times, P2, (K2tog, P2) 12 times, K2tog*, work to third marker, rep from * to *, work to end—350 (382) sts.

Next row (RS): Work to 17 sts past first marker, put sts just worked on holder for right front, BO 35 sts, work to end.

Next row: Work to 17 sts past marker, put sts just worked on holder for left front, BO 35 sts, work to end—128 (144) sts on back and 76 (84) sts on each front.

Back

Work 14 rows on back in established ribbing, keeping first and last st as K1.

Work smock patt on RS rows of back as follows.

Next row: K1, (K2, P2) 3 times, smock st, P2, K2, P2, (K6, P2) 10 (12) times, K2, P2, smock st, (P2, K2) 3 times, K1.

Work 13 rows in established ribbing.

Next row: K1, (K2, P2) 4 times, (smock st, P2,) twice, (K6, P2) 8 (10) times, (smock st, P2) twice, (K2, P2) 3 times, K2, K1.

Work 13 rows in established ribbing.

Next row: K1, (K2, P2) 3 times, (smock st, P2) 3 times, K2, P2, (K6, P2) 6 (8) times, K2, P2, (smock st, P2) 3 times, (K2, P2) twice, K2, K1.

Work 13 rows in established ribbing.

Next row: K1, (K2, P2) 4 times, (smock st, P2) 4 times, (K6, P2) 4 (6) times, (smock st, P2) 4 times, (K2, P2) 3 times, K2, K1.

Work 9 rows in established ribbing.

Next row: K1, (K2, P2) 3 times, (smock st, P2) 5 times, K2, P2, (K6, P2) 2 (4) times, K2, P2, (smock st, P2) 5 times, (K2, P2) twice, K2, K1.

Work 5 rows in established ribbing.

Next row for Small/Medium: K1, (K2, P2) 4 times, (smock st, P2) 12 times, (K2, P2) 3 times, K2, K1.

Next row for Large/Extra Large: K1, (K2, P2) 4 times, (smock st, P2) 6 times, (K6, P2) twice, (smock st, P2) 6 times, (K2, P2) 3 times, K2, K1.

For all sizes, work 5 rows in established ribbing.

Next row: K1, (K2, P2) 3 times, (smock st, P2) 13 (15) times, (K2, P2) twice, K2, K1.

Work 3 (5) rows in established ribbing. Leave sts on holder.

Fronts

Right front: With WS facing you, join yarn at armhole edge. Work 13 rows in established ribbing.

Next row (RS): K1, (K2, P2) 5 times, (K6, P2) 4 (5) times, K2, P2, smock st, (P2, K2) 3 times, K1.

Cont working smock patt same as left half of back until right front measures same as back. Don't forget second buttonhole, 3" from the first one. Put sts on holder while you work left front.

Left front: With RS facing you, join yarn at armhole edge. Work 14 rows in ribbing.

Next row (RS): K1, (K2, P2) 3 times, smock st, P2, K2, (P2, K6) 4 (5) times, (P2, K2) 5 times, K1.

Cont working smock patt same as right half of back until left front measures same as back.

When fronts measure same as back, join shoulders with 3-needle BO (page 13), leaving 32 sts on each front for collar. Put right collar sts on st holder.

Collar: Join yarn to outer edge of collar, working toward neck. Work collar patt (4 rows of rev St st alternating with 4 rows of St st), joining collar to back as follows.

Row 1: Work to last st, sl the next 2 sts (last st from needle and first st from holder), K2tog. Turn.

Row 2: Sl 1, work to end.

Rep these 2 rows until all sts from back have been joined to collar. Join with Kitchener st (page 12) to other end of collar.

Sleeves

With RS facing you, starting from lower corner at armhole, PU 118 sts.

Next row (WS): (P6, K2) 14 times, P6.

Work 5 (6)" in established ribbing, ending with WS row.

Work smock patt on RS rows as follows.

Next row: (K6, P2) 6 times, (K2, P2) twice, smock st, P2, (K2, P2) twice, (K6, P2) 5 times, K6.

Work 9 rows in established ribbing.

Next row: K1, K2tog, K3, P2, (K6, P2) 4 times, (K2, P2) 3 times, (smock st, P2) twice, (K2, P2) 3 times, (K6, P2) 4 times, K3, K2tog, K1.

Work 9 rows in established ribbing.

Next row: K1, K2tog, K2, P2, (K6, P2) 3 times, (K2, P2) twice, (smock st, P2) 5 times, (K2, P2) twice, (K6, P2) 3 times, K2, K2tog, K1.

Work 9 rows in established ribbing.

Next row: K1, K2tog, K1, P2, K6, (P2, K2) twice, P2, (smock st, P2) 9 times, (K2, P2) twice, K6, P2, K1, K2tog, K1.

Work 9 rows in established ribbing.

Next row: K3, P2, (smock st, P2) 13 times, K3.

Work 5 rows in established ribbing.

Next row: *K1, (smock st, P2) 13 times, smock st, K1.

Work 5 rows in established ribbing.

Next row: K3, P2, (smock st, P2) 13 times, K3.*

Work from * to * one more time.

Next row: K1, K2tog, work in established ribbing to last 3 sts, K2tog, K1.

Work 1½" in established ribbing. BO in patt.

Finishing

Sew up sleeve and underarm seam. Sew on buttons.

Finishing time: Approx 40 minutes.

Block garment to finished measurements.

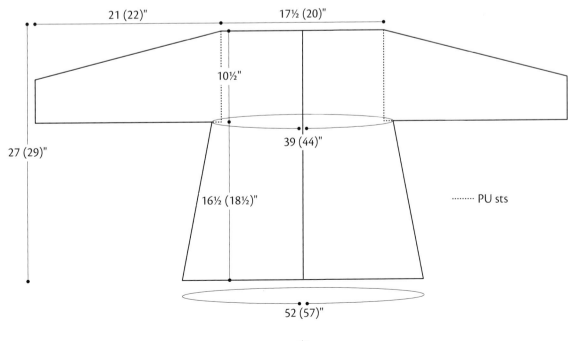

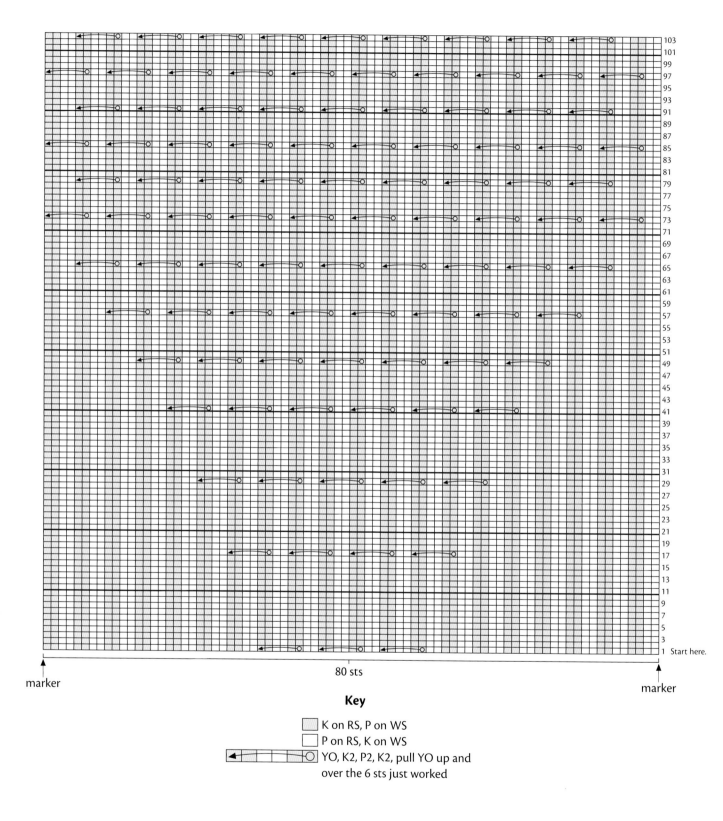

80 sts

marker

marker

Key

K on RS, P on WS

P on RS, K on WS

YO, K2, P2, K2, pull YO up and
over the 6 sts just worked

Three-Directional Pullover

Worked in soft yellow, with sweet buttoned cuff details, this sweater has it all. The sweater is named for the ribbed pattern, which goes vertically at the bottom, diagonally on the body, and horizontally on the sleeves.

Skill level: Intermediate ■■■□

Sizes: Small (Medium, Large, Extra Large)

Finished bust: 37 (42, 48, 53)" in pattern

Finished length: 20 (22, 24, 25)"

Materials

11 (11,12,13) skeins of Cashsoft Baby DK from Rowan Classic Yarns (57% merino, 33% microfiber, 10% cashmere; 50 g; 130 m/142 yds) in color 802 **3**

2 size 6 (4 mm) circular needles (16" and 32" long) or size to obtain gauge

4 buttons, ½" diameter

2 stitch markers

2 stitch holders

Gauge

22 sts and 32 rows = 4" in St st

Front

Garment is worked in one piece from front to back.

CO 112 (128, 144, 160) sts.

Vertical Ribbing

Row 1 (WS): K2, (P4, K4) to the last 6 sts, end with P4, K2.

Row 2: Knit the knit sts and purl the purl sts as they face you.

Work rows 1 and 2 for 3½", ending with WS row. On last row, work 56 (64, 72, 80) sts, pm, finish row.

Diagonal Ribbing

Next RS row: P1, (K4, P4) across to 7 sts before marker, K4, P3, sm, P3, K4, (P4, K4) across to last st, P1. As you can see, the second half is a mirror image of the first. This makes it easier for you to understand the flow of sts.

Next and all WS rows: Knit the knit sts and purl the purl sts as they face you.

Next RS row: (K4, P4) to center, sm, (P4, K4) to end. Get the picture? Sts move diagonally to right and left by 1 st on every RS row.

Work in established patt until piece measures 12 (14, 15, 16)" from beg, ending with WS row.

Sleeves

Pm to indicate beg of sleeve at underarm. At each end, use provisional crochet-ch CO (page 10) to CO 69 (75, 69, 75) sts, pm, then CO 15 more sts for cuffs—84 (90, 84, 90) sts total for each sleeve.

Work horizontal ribbing on cuff and sleeve sts as indicated below and AT THE SAME TIME work diagonal patt as established.

Cuff patt: Working on 15 sts at cuff, on next RS row and beg with a purl row, work 2 rows of rev St st alternating with 2 rows of St st.

Sleeve patt: Working on sts between marker at cuff and marker at underarm, beg with purl row, work 4 rows of rev St st alternating with 4 rows of St st.

Work cuff and sleeve patts as established, while cont to move diagonal ribbing as established in/out toward sleeve by 1 st every RS row, until sleeve measures 7½ (7½, 8½, 8½)" from provisional CO. There should be 2 knit or 2 purl sts on either side of center marker, if not, work additional rows until you have 2 matching sts on either side of center marker.

Next row: Work in established sleeve and diagonal patt to center 44 sts, pm at each end of the 44 sts and work in established 4/4 ribbing, finish row in established diagonal and sleeve patt. Work a total of 4 rows in this manner.

Next row: Work to neck, put 44 neck sts on holder, join second ball of yarn and finish row.

Work a total of 8 rows in established patt on each side. This marks the halfway point of sweater, pm on last row.

Back

Next row: Work to neck. Using provisional crochet-ch CO (page 10), CO 44 sts, work to end of row with single ball of yarn. Cut extra ball.

Cont in established patt, but now reverse diagonal patt by moving the diagonal toward the center back by 1 st, and inc the sleeve patt by 1 st on every RS row.

When sleeve measures same from halfway point to CO row, join sleeve seams as follows. Remove provisional CO, put sts on needle. *BO first 15 sts from front needle for cuff (put 15 sts from back needle on holder). Use 3-needle BO (page 13) to BO rem sleeve sts. Work to end of row. Turn*. Rep from * to *.

Cont in reverse diagonal patt until back measures same as front to start of ribbing. Work vertical 4/4 ribbing same as beg ribbing for 3½". BO all sts in patt.

Finishing

Neck: Join yarn, keeping in 4/4 ribbing, PU 44 sts from provisional CO, 4 sts from shoulder, 44 sts from holder, and 4 sts from shoulder—96 sts. Join into rnd, pm, and work in established 4/4 ribbing for 10 rnds. BO in patt.

Cuffs: Join yarn to 15 sts on holder. Knit 1 row. On next row, (K4, YO, K2tog) twice, K3. Knit 1 row. BO sts. Attach buttons.

Sew side seams.

Finishing time: Approx 30 minutes.

Block garment to finished measurements.

Diagonal ribbing is worked into the sleeves.

Detail on the neck and shoulders

Cuff ribbing and buttons

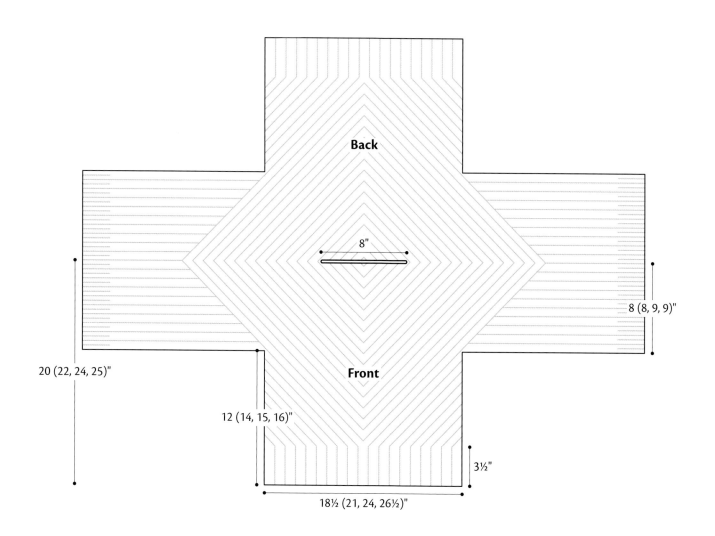

Cabled Summer Top

Different sizes of cables create this shapely sweater.
Tapered at the waist, this sweater's scalloped bottom
and back neck edge add to its charm.

Skill level: Intermediate ◼◼◼◻

Sizes: Small (Medium, Large, Extra Large)

Finished bust: 33 (38, 43, 48)" in pattern

Finished length: 20 (20, 22½, 24)"

Materials

6 (7, 8, 10) skeins of Natural Focus Ecologie Cotton
from Nashua Handknits (100% cotton; 50 g; 100
m/110 yds) in color 77 **3**

Size 7 (4.5 mm) needles or size to obtain gauge

Cable needle

Gauge

24 sts = 4" in St st

Cable Abbreviations

Small cable (C6F). Sl 3 sts to cn and hold in front, K3,
K3 from cn.

Large cable (C8F). Sl 4 sts to cn and hold in front, K4,
K4 from cn.

Back

Garment is worked in one piece from back to front.

CO 102 (120, 138, 156) sts.

Bottom Detail

Rows 1, 3, and 5 (WS): Purl

Rows 2 and 4: (P3, K6) across to last 3 sts, P3.

Row 6: (P3, C6F) across to last 3 sts, P3.

Work 18 (18, 24, 24) rows of small cable patt.

The detail of the small cables at the bottom edge

Back view of the cables

Neck detail and center cable

Cable worked on the sleeve cap

Body

Beg large cable patt.

Rows 1, 3, 5, 7, 9, and 11 (WS): Purl.

Rows 2, 4, 6, 8, and 10: P1, (P1, K8) across to last 2 sts, P2.

Row 12: P1, (P1, C8F) to last 2 sts, P2.

Work rows 1–12 for 59 rows.

Row 60 (row 12 of large cable): P2, C8F, (P1, K8) 3 (4, 5, 6) times, (P1, C8F) 3 times, (P1, K8) 3 (4, 5, 6) times, P1, C8F, P2.

Cont in established patt, working cable cross only on first cable, on middle 3 cables, and on last cable for a total of 3 (3, 4, 5) large cable reps.

Cap Sleeves

On next RS row, use knitted CO (page 9) to CO 3 sts at each end for sleeves—108 (126, 144, 162) sts. (For longer sleeves you could CO 12 sts at each end and work another cable patt for sleeve.) Keeping first and last 5 sts in purl garter, work 47 rows in established patt.

Back neck patt: P5, C8F, (P1, K8) 1 (2, 3, 4) times, P2, C6F, (P3, C6F) 6 times, P2, (K8, P1) 1 (2, 3, 4) times, C8F, P5.

Cont cable patts as set for 7 (7, 10, 10) more rows.

Next row: Work in established patt across 33 (42, 50, 59) sts, BO 42 (42, 44, 44) sts, finish row in established patt. Mark this row as halfway point.

Front

Join second ball of yarn for right shoulder and work patt as set until one more small cable has been crossed, followed by a WS row.

Next RS row (inc): Work to the 2 purl sts before small cable, P1, M1, P1, K8, P2. Second half: P2, K8, P1, M1, P1, work to end. Working patt as established, work inc on every 4 rows 7 (7, 8, 8) times, then EOR 14 times, incorporating incs into K8, P1 patt.

AT THE SAME TIME when sleeve cap measures same as halfway point to beg of sleeve, BO 3 sts at beg of next 2 rows (or BO 12 sts if you made longer sleeves). After all incs are finished, join front by working across row with 1 yarn. Cut second ball of yarn.

Work rem patt as established, except work 1 large cable cross at each side and 1 large cable cross at center front.

Cont until piece measures same as beg to start of large cable patt. Work large cable patt across as for back, beg with row 12. Cont to match the back, start small cable patt at row 6. When work measures same as back, end with row 3 of small cable patt. BO in patt.

Finishing

Sew side seams and small portion of underarm.

Finishing time: Approx 20 minutes.

Block garment to finished measurements.

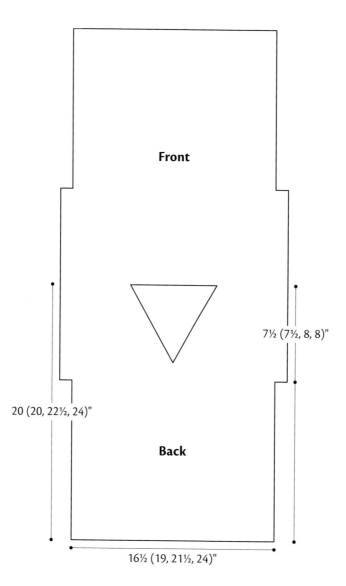

Front

7½ (7½, 8, 8)"

20 (20, 22½, 24)"

Back

16½ (19, 21½, 24)"

Easy Breezy Top

Wear this cool top on a warm summer day,
or as a vest on cooler days.

Skill level: Beginner ■□□□

Sizes: Small (Medium, Large, Extra Large)

Finished bust: 34 (36, 43½, 47½)"

Finished length: 19 (21, 23, 23)"

Materials

6 (7, 8, 10) skeins of Snuggly Baby Bamboo from
   Sirdar (80% bamboo, 20% wool; 50 g; 95 m/104
   yds) in color 132 [3]

Size 6 (4 mm) needles or size to obtain gauge

3 stitch markers

Gauge

24 sts = 4" in St st

Back

Garment is worked in one piece from back to front.

CO 103 (109, 131, 143) sts.

Bottom Edge

Row 1 (WS): K1, purl to last st, K1.

Row 2 (RS): (K1, P1) across to last st, K1.

Work rows 1 and 2 for 2", ending with row 1.

Body

Next RS row: (K1, P1) 3 times, knit to last 6 sts, (P1,
   K1) 3 times.

Next WS row: K1, purl to last st, K1.

Work last 2 rows until piece measures 8 (9, 10, 10)"
   from beg. On last row, work 51 (54, 65, 71) sts,
   mark next st, finish row.

Ribbing in V patt: On next RS row, work to 1 st before
   marked st, P1, K1, P1, finish row in established patt.
   Inc number of sts in yoke ribbing on every 4th row
   by working 2 more sts in patt on each side, creating
   a V patt. For example, on next 3 rows, work in patt.
   On next RS row, work to 3 sts before center, (P1,

Ribbing at the bottom edge

Ribbing pattern at the V-neck

K1) 3 times, P1, finish row. Work in patt, remem-
bering to inc sts in yoke ribbing on every 4th row,
until piece measures 14 (15, 17, 17)", ending with
WS row.

Divide for V-Neck

On next RS row, work in established patt to center st,
   join another ball of yarn, BO 1 st, finish row—51

Armhole ribbing

Detail of the side slit and ribbing pattern at the side seam

(54, 65, 71) sts each side. With separate balls of yarn, work each side, cont established V patt until piece measures 19 (21, 23, 23)" from beg. Mark last row as halfway point.

Front

From now on reverse the V patt by reducing 2 patt sts at each end on a RS row, every 4 rows. When piece measures 7 (7, 8, 8)" from halfway point, join pieces by working across with one ball, inc 1 st in the middle, and cut the second ball. When V patt comes to the last 3 sts, work in St st to match back. Start bottom edge 2" before the total length. Work bottom edge as for back for 2". BO in patt.

Finishing

Sew up side seams, leaving 2" side slits open at bottom, and leaving armholes open as desired. After sewing side seam for several inches, try top on and decide if you want to sew further or leave a larger opening to make it more like a vest.

Finishing time: Approx 15 minutes.

Block garment to finished measurements.

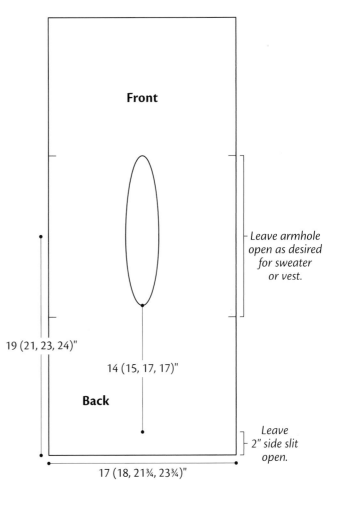

Front

Leave armhole open as desired for sweater or vest.

19 (21, 23, 24)"

14 (15, 17, 17)"

Back

Leave 2" side slit open.

17 (18, 21¾, 23¾)"

Openwork Projects

Openwork can make garments lighter in weight, more feminine, and faster to knit. It is also a quick and easy way to add ease and a flattering shape to your garments.

How To

Openwork. There are several ways you can create light and airy knitted fabrics. Using a larger-than-normal needle size for the yarn will make the stitches larger, resulting in more space between the stitches. Alternating different yarns on different needle sizes can also create openness. Dropping stitches and allowing them to run for several inches will also open up the knitting.

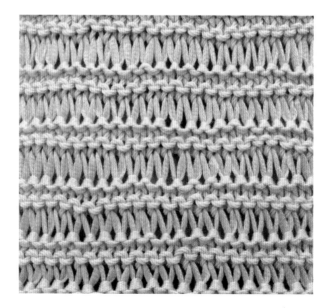

Featherlight Cardigan, page 66

Quick and Easy Top, page 70

Drop-Stitch Vest, page 72

Featherlight Cardigan

This cardigan feels like cotton candy,
but it still keeps you warm.

Skill level: Easy ◐■□□

Sizes: Small (Medium, Large)

Finished bust: 35½ (37½, 40½)"

Finished length: 19 (20, 23)"

Materials

A 1 (2, 2) skeins of Lacey Lamb from Jade Sapphire (100% extrafine Lambswool; 825 yds) in color 02 【1】

B 3 (4, 4) skeins of Kidsilk Haze from Rowan (70% super kid mohair, 30% silk; 25 g; 210 m/229 yds) in color 634 【1】

Size 5 (3.5 mm) circular needle (24" long)

Size 7 (4.5 mm) circular needle (29" long) or size to obtain gauge

Size 8 (5 mm) circular needles (29" long)

5 (6, 7) buttons, approx ½" diameter

3 stitch holders

4 stitch markers

Gauge

24 sts = 4" in St st with 1 strand each of A and B held tog on size 7 needle

Twisted Cable Pattern

Right twist (RT): Knit 2 sts tog, don't take st off needle, knit first st again and take both sts off needle.

Row 1 (RS): K3, (RT, K2) to last 3 sts, K3.

Rows 2, 4, and 6: K3, purl to last 3 sts, K3 .

Rows 3 and 7: Knit.

Row 5: K3, (K2, RT) to last 3 sts, K3.

Row 8: K3, purl to last 3 sts, K3.

Rep rows 1–8.

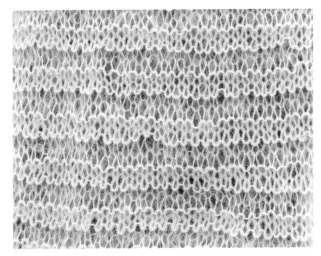

Detail of the bottom garter-stitch pattern in alternating yarns

Body

Garment is worked in one piece to armholes.

With size 8 needle and using 2 strands of A for thumb yarn and 1 strand of B over index finger, use decorative CO (page 9) to CO 218 (230, 250) sts. Cut 1 strand of A. Working with 1 strand of A or B, work in garter st, alternating 2 rows of single-strand B and 2 rows of single-strand A. Carry yarn not in use loosely up front, being careful to keep edges neat. Work until piece measures 4 (4, 5)".

Change to size 7 needle, and using 1 strand of A and B held tog, work rows 1–8 of twisted cable patt once, AT THE SAME TIME work buttonhole on row 5 (RS) as follows: K2, YO, K2tog. Work rows 1–4 of twisted cable patt once more.

Keeping 3-st garter at each end, work in St st until piece measures 6 (7, 8½)" above garter-st border, ending with WS row. Rep buttonhole row on first 4 sts as above every 3" for a total of 5 (6, 7) buttonholes.

Shape armholes: On next RS row, K50 (53, 57), BO 12 (12, 14) sts, K94 (100, 108), BO 12 (12, 14) sts, K50 (53, 57). Leave all sts on holder or needle (leave tail long enough to work across left front when joining pieces).

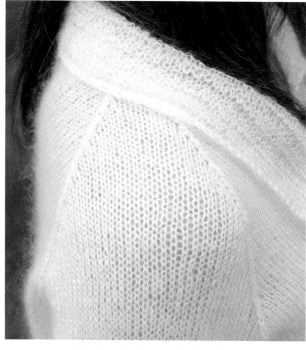

Raglan shaping at the shoulders

Detail of the collar in alternating yarns

Sleeves

With size 7 needle, and using 2 strands of A for thumb yarn and 1 strand of B over index finger, use decorative CO to CO 68 (68, 78) sts. Cut 1 strand of A. Working with 1 strand each of A and B held tog, work twisted cable patt for 9 rows. Work in St st, inc 1 st at each end on next row and then every 1" a total of 4 (4, 5) times—76 (76, 88) sts. Work incs 1 st in from the edge to make finishing easier.

Work even until sleeve measures 7 (7, 8)" from beg, ending with WS row.

BO 6 (6, 7) sts at beg of next 2 rows—64 (64, 74) sts.

Knit 1 row.

Join Sleeves to Body

With WS facing you, work across left front sts (with tail from armhole shaping), pm; now with main yarn, work across sleeve sts, pm, work across back sts, pm, work across sleeve sts, pm, work across right front sts—322 (334, 370) sts.

Work 2 rows. Remember garter edges and rem butonholes.

Raglan decs: *Work to 1 st before marker, remove marker, sl2tog kw-K1-p2sso*. You can replace marker before last st, but after a while the decs become obvious. Rep from * to * across. Work dec as set on EOR until piece measures 5 (5, 6)" from beg of raglan shaping (measure vertically, not on diagonal line).

Shape neck: BO 6 sts at beg of next 4 rows, 5 sts at beg of next 4 rows. Cont even at neck edge, and work raglan dec as established until last front st is worked into raglan. Cut yarn. Leave rem sts on needle.

Finishing

Collar: With size 5 needle and 1 strand each of yarn
A and B held tog, PU 32 (38, 41) sts from front
neck to shoulder, 8 (2, 4) from sleeve, knit across
38 back sts, 8 (2, 4) from other sleeve, PU 32 (38,
41) sts from other side—118 (118, 128) sts. Work 8
rows in garter st beg with knit row, working 1 more
buttonhole on 4th row if necessary. Change to size
8 needle. Work in garter st until collar measures 3",
alternating 2 rows of single-strand B and single-
strand A. BO pw on WS row with 2 strands of A
and 1 strand of B held tog.

Sew up sleeve and underarm seam. Sew on buttons.

Finishing time: Approx 30 minutes.

Block garment to finished measurements.

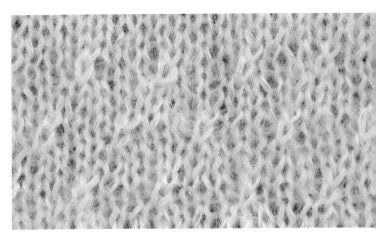

Twisted cable pattern

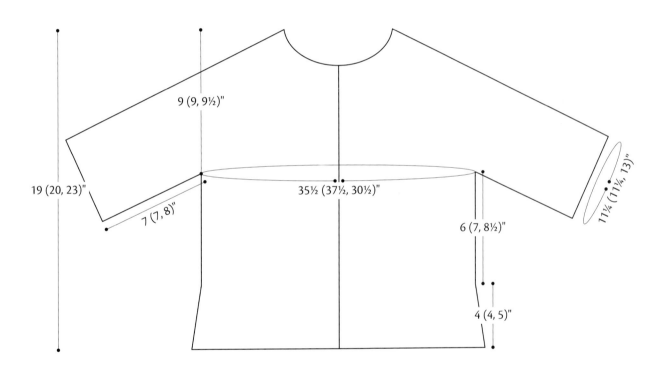

9 (9, 9½)"

19 (20, 23)"

7 (7, 8)"

35½ (37½, 30½)"

6 (7, 8½)"

11¼ (11¼, 13)"

4 (4, 5)"

Quick and Easy Top

This garment is worked in two different yarn textures in matching colors. The openwork pattern at the bottom adds a slight A-line shape.

Skill level: Beginner ■□□□

Sizes: Extra Small (Small, Medium, Large)

Finished bust: 33 (36½, 40½, 44)"

Finished length: 19 (21, 23, 23)"

Materials

A 4 (5, 5, 7) skeins of Sky from Tahki Stacy Charles (100% cotton; 50 g; 92 yds/85 m) in color 2 **4**

B 2 (2, 3, 3) skeins of Bamboo Tape from Rowan (100% bamboo; 50 g; 82 yds/75 m) in color 705 **4**

Size 8 (5 mm) needles or size to obtain gauge

Size 17 (12 mm) needles

2 stitch markers

2 stitch holders

Gauge

17 sts = 4" in St st with A on smaller needles

Back and Front

With size 8 needles and A, CO 70 (78, 86, 94) sts. Knit 5 rows.

Openwork Pattern

Carry yarn not in use loosely up sides.

Row 1 (RS): With size 17 needle and B, knit.

Row 2: With size 8 needle and B, knit

Rows 3 and 4: With size 8 needle and A, knit.

Work rows 1–4 a total of 8 (8, 8, 9) times. Cut B.

Piece should measure approx 9½ (9½, 9½, 11¾)".

Body

With size 8 needles and A, cont in St st until piece measures 9½ (11½, 13½, 13½)" from beg of St st.

Knit 2 rows with A. Work rows 1–4 of openwork patt. Knit 2 rows with A.

Neck opening: With A, K20 (22, 25, 28), BO 30 (34, 36, 38) sts, knit to end. Place sts on holders.

Work second piece same as first.

Join shoulders with 3-needle BO and A.

Cap Sleeves

Mark 7 (8, 9, 9)" down from shoulder seam on front and back. With size 8 needles and A, PU 58 (64, 72) sts between markers.

Knit 1 row with A.

Work rows 1–4 of openwork patt. Cut B.

Knit 2 more rows in A. BO all sts.

Finishing

Sew up side seams, being careful not to pull too tight.

Finishing time: Approx 30 minutes.

Block garment to finished measurements.

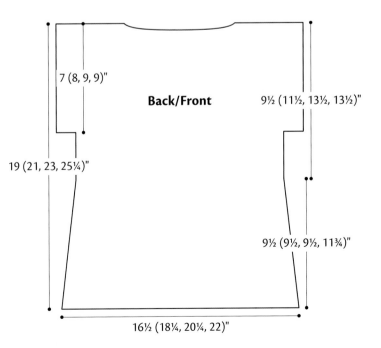

7 (8, 9, 9)"

19 (21, 23, 25¼)"

Back/Front

9½ (11½, 13½, 13½)"

9½ (9½, 9½, 11¾)"

16½ (18¼, 20¼, 22)"

Drop-Stitch Vest

Graduated dropped stitches add flair
and ease to this versatile vest.

Skill level: Easy ◐■☐☐

Sizes: Small (Medium, Large)

Finished bust: 35 (38, 41)" in pattern

Finished length: 23½ (25½, 27)"

Materials

MC 6 (7, 8) skeins of NaturLin from Berroco (45% linen, 55% rayon; 50 g; 115 yds/106 m) in color 6303 Oat ③

CC 1 skein of NaturLin Berroco in color 6332 Denim

Size 6 (4 mm) circular needle (32" long) or size to obtain gauge

Size 7 (4.5 mm) circular needle (32" long)

6 small beads for end of twisted cord

21 (23, 25) stitch markers

3 stitch holders

Gauge

24 sts = 4" in St st on smaller needle

Body

Vest is worked in one piece to armholes.

With CC and larger needle, CO 249 (271, 293) sts. Knit 1 row (WS). Cut CC.

Change to smaller needle and MC; work bottom detail as follows.

Row 1 (RS): (K1, P1) twice, K10, pm, (K11, pm) 20 (22, 24) times, K11, (P1, K1) twice.

Row 2: K2, P1, K1, purl to last 4 sts, K1, P1, K2.

Rep these 2 rows until piece measures 2½ (2½, 3)" from beg, ending with WS row.

Next row (RS): Work to first marker, remove marker, drop next st (don't do anything with it yet), work to next marker, remove marker, drop next st, work across to last 2 markers, drop sts after markers, remove these 2 markers, and work to end.

Drop stitch detail at the bottom of the vest

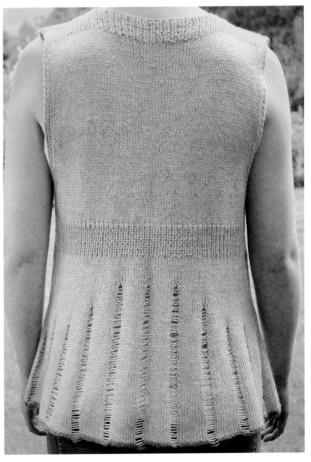

Back with ribbed waistband and shoulders

Detail of the armhole

A loop and a twisted cord make a nice closure.

Work 1" in St st, keeping established K1, P1 ribbing at each end. Rep as before, remove markers and drop sts after next 2 markers and the last 2 markers. Cont in this manner, dropping sts until you have 3 markers left for Small and Medium, 5 markers for Large. Work 1" between dropped sts. Drop the last set of sts after the rem markers—228 (248, 268) sts.

Work in St st until piece measures 10 (11, 11)" from beg, ending with WS row.

Mark side seams on next row, K59 (64, 69), pm, work K1, P1 ribbing on 110 (120, 130) sts, pm, finish row.

Cont in established patt for 1½ (2, 2½)", ending with WS row.

Next row: Work to 5 sts before first marker, work established ribbing over next 10 sts, work in St st to 5 sts before next marker, work established ribbing over next 10 sts, finish row.

Work in established patt for 1" ending on WS row.

Front neck shaping: On next RS row, work 4 sts in ribbing, ssk, work in established patt to last 6 sts , K2tog, work 4 sts in ribbing. Work neck decs every 4 rows a total of 19 (19, 20) times. AT THE SAME TIME, divide for back and fronts.

Divide for back and fronts (AT THE SAME TIME as neck shaping): When underarm rib measures 1½ (2, 2½)", ending with WS row, work to second marker, turn. Leave front sts on holders.

Body

Next RS row (double dec): Working on back only, work 5 sts in established ribbing, sl2 kw-K1-p2sso, work to last 8 sts, K3tog, work 5 sts in established ribbing.

Work 1 WS row.

Rep double dec row on next RS row.

Work 1 WS row.

Next RS row (single dec): Work 5 sts in established ribbing, ssk, work to last 7 sts, K2tog, work 5 sts in established ribbing.

Rep single dec row every 4 rows a total of 4 (4, 5) times.

Work even until armhole measures 9 (9, 9½)".

Work K1, P1 ribbing across all sts for 1½". Put sts on st holder.

Fronts

Left Front

With RS facing you, attach yarn at armhole edge, work 5 sts in established ribbing, sl2 kw-K1-p2sso, finish row. Work double dec at armhole on EOR a total of 4 (4, 5) times.

Next RS row: Work 4 sts in established ribbing, ssk, finish row. Work armhole dec every 4 rows a total of 6 times. Be sure to cont with front neck dec as established. Cont until front measures same as back.

Right Front

With WS facing you, attach yarn at armhole edge, work 5 sts in established ribbing at armhole and 4 sts in ribbing at neck. Reversing shaping, work dec as for left front, but work K2tog at neck edge and K3tog at armhole edge.

Finishing

Join first shoulder with 3-needle BO (page 13), then BO back sts, finish with 3-needle BO on second shoulder.

Loop and twisted cord: With CC make a crochet-ch loop for closure for one side.

Make twisted cord as follows: Cut 3 pieces of yarn approx 15" long. Hold the 3 strands tog, one end in each hand. Twist the strands until they fold in half when you release the tension slightly. With the cord now in half, tie a knot about 2" from loose ends. Insert the folded end into a st opposite the ch loop and pull loose ends through (like when making fringe). Put a bead near the end of each strand of yarn and secure with a knot below. Pull cord through ch loop to close.

Unravel dropped sts to end and block vest, straightening the floats.

Done! No sewing!

Finishing time: 0 minutes.

Block garment to finished measurements.

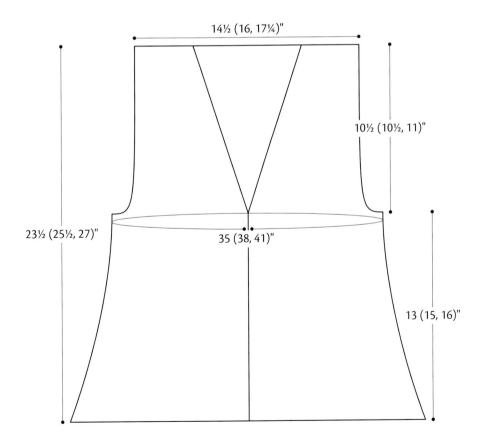

14½ (16, 17¼)"

10½ (10½, 11)"

23½ (25½, 27)"

35 (38, 41)"

13 (15, 16)"

Abbreviations and Glossary

approx	approximately		**rem**	remain(ing)
beg	begin(ning)		**rep(s)**	repeat(s)
BO	bind off		**rev St st**	reverse stockinette stitch: purl on right side, knit on wrong side
CC	contrasting color			
ch	chain(s)		**RH**	right hand
cn	cable needle(s)		**rnd(s)**	round(s)
CO	cast on		**RS**	right side
cont	continue(ing)(s)		**sc**	single crochet
dec	decrease(ing)(s)		**sl2 kw-K1-p2sso**	
EOR	every other row			slip 2 stitches one at a time knitwise, knit 1 stitch, pass the 2 slipped stitches over the knit stitch; left slanting double decrease (page 11)
g	gram(s)			
inc	increase(ing)(s)			
K	knit			
K2tog	knit 2 stitches together; right slant single decrease (page 10)		**sl2tog kw-K1-p2sso**	
				slip 2 stitches together knitwise, knit 1 stitch, pass the 2 slipped stitches over the knit stitch; centered double decrease (page 11)
K3tog	knit 3 stitches together; right slant double decrease (page 10)			
			sl	slip
kw	knitwise		**sm**	slip marker
LH	left hand		**ssk**	slip, slip, knit; left slant single decrease (page 10)
m	meter(s)			
M1	make 1 stitch (see page 10)		**st(s)**	stitch(es)
MC	main color		**St st**	stockinette stitch: Back and forth, knit on right side, purl on wrong side. In the rnd, knit every round
mm	millimeter(s)			
oz	ounce(s)			
P	purl		**tbl**	through back loop(s)
patt	pattern(s)		**tog**	together
pm	place marker		**WS**	wrong side
PU	pick up and knit		**wyif**	with yarn in front
pw	purlwise		**yd(s)**	yard(s)
			YO(s)	yarn over(s)

Useful Information

Metric Conversions

Yards x .91 = meters

Meters x 1.09 = yards

Grams x .035 = ounces

Ounces x 28.35 = grams

Standard Yarn-Weight System

Yarn-Weight Symbol and Category Names	1 SUPER FINE	2 FINE	3 LIGHT	4 MEDIUM	5 BULKY	6 SUPER BULKY
Types of Yarns in Category	Sock, Fingering, Baby	Sport, Baby	DK, Light Worsted	Worsted, Afghan, Aran	Chunky, Craft, Rug	Bulky, Roving
Knit Gauge Ranges in Stockinette Stitch to 4"	27 to 32 sts	23 to 26 sts	21 to 24 sts	16 to 20 sts	12 to 15 sts	6 to 11 sts
Recommended Needle in U.S. Size Range	1 to 3	3 to 5	5 to 7	7 to 9	9 to 11	11 and larger
Recommended Needle in Metric Size Range	2.25 to 3.25 mm	3.25 to 3.75 mm	3.75 to 4.5 mm	4.5 to 5.5 mm	5.5 to 8 mm	8 mm and larger

Skill Levels

■□□□ **Beginner:** Projects for first-time knitters using basic knit and purl stitches; minimal shaping.

■■□□ **Easy:** Projects using basic stitches, repetitive stitch patterns, and simple color changes; simple shaping and finishing.

■■■□ **Intermediate:** Projects using a variety of stitches, such as basic cables and lace, simple intarsia, and techniques for double-pointed needles and knitting in the round; midlevel shaping.

■■■■ **Experienced:** Projects using advanced techniques and stitches, such as short rows, Fair Isle, more intricate intarsia, cables, lace patterns, and numerous color changes.

Yarn Resources

Refer to the following websites for information on the yarns used in this book.

Berroco
www.berroco.com
NaturLin

Cascade Yarns
www.cascadeyarns.com
Bollicine Dolly

Muench Yarns
www.muenchyarns.com
GGH Tajmahal
Lana Grossa Merino Big

Knitting Fever
www.knittingfever.com
Sirdar Snuggly Baby Bamboo, Sirdar Sublime

Tahki Stacy Charles
www.tahkistacycharles.com
Sky

Westminster Fibers
www.westminsterfibers.com
Gedifra Extra Soft Merino

Nashua Handknits Natural Focus Ecologie Cotton

Rowan Calmer, Rowan Bamboo Tape, Rowan Kidsilk Haze

Rowan Classic Yarns Cashsoft Baby DK

Schachenmayr Micro Bamboo, Schachenmayr Catania

Jade Sapphire
www.jadesapphire.com
4-ply Mongolian Cashmere, Lacey Lamb

About the Author

Eva Wiechmann has been the owner of Eva's Needlework in Thousand Oaks, California, since 1987, where she enjoys creating patterns for her many local customers. Every time a shipment of wonderful new yarns arrives she cannot wait to get her needles clicking and the creative juices flowing.

In her spare time, Eva loves running. She has completed five Los Angeles marathons. The best ideas come to her while running the trails in her neighborhood early in the morning. Nothing, however, can compare to the joy her four grandchildren give her. "Every grandmother knows what I am talking about," she says.

Eva is the author of *Pursenalities, Pursenality Plus,* and *Crocheted Pursenalities.*

Knitting and Crochet Titles

ACCESSORIES

Crocheted Pursenalities
Crocheted Socks!
Kitty Knits
Pursenalities
Pursenality Plus
Stitch Style: Mittens
Toe-Up Techniques for Hand-Knit Socks,
Revised Edition

BABIES, CHILDREN, & TOYS

Gigi Knits…and Purls
Knitted Finger Puppets
Knitting with Gigi
Too Cute!

CROCHET

365 Crochet Stitches a Year: Perpetual Calendar
Amigurumi World
A to Z of Crochet
First Crochet

LITTLE BOX SERIES

The Little Box of Crocheted Gifts
The Little Box of Crocheted Throws
The Little Box of Knitted Gifts
The Little Box of Knitted Throws
The Little Box of Socks

KNITTING

200 Knitted Blocks
365 Knitting Stitches a Year: Perpetual Calendar
All about Knitting
A to Z of Knitting
Beyond Wool
Cable Confidence
Casual, Elegant Knits
Chic Knits
Fair Isle Sweaters Simplified
Handknit Skirts
Knit One, Stripe Too
The Knitter's Book of Finishing Techniques
Ocean Breezes
Simple Gifts for Dog Lovers
Simple Stitches—*NEW!*
Skein for Skein
Special Little Knits from Just One Skein
Stripes, Stripes, Stripes
Together or Separate
Top Down Sweaters
Wrapped in Comfort

SOCK KNITTING

Knitting Circles around Socks
More Sensational Knitted Socks
Sensational Knitted Socks
Stitch Style: Socks

Our books are available at bookstores and your favorite craft, fabric, and yarn retailers. If you don't see the title you're looking for, visit us at
www.martingale-pub.com or contact us at:

1-800-426-3126

International: 1-425-483-3313
Fax: 1-425-486-7596 • **Email:** info@martingale-pub.com

Martingale®
& COMPANY

America's Best-Loved Craft & Hobby Books®
America's Best-Loved Knitting Books®

1/09 Knit